You've Got to Reach Them to Teach Them

MaryKim Schreck

Hard Facts About the Soft Skills of Student Engagement

Solution Tree | Press

a division of
Solution Tree

555 North Morton Street
Bloomington, IN 47404
800.733.6786 (toll free) / 812.336.7700
FAX: 812.336.7790

email: info@solution-tree.com
solution-tree.com

Visit **go.solution-tree.com/instruction** to download the reproducibles and access live links to the websites in this book.

Printed in the United States of America

14 13 12 11   2 3 4 5

FSC
Mixed Sources
Product group from well-managed
forests and other controlled sources
Cert no. SW-COC-002283
www.fsc.org
© 1996 Forest Stewardship Council

Library of Congress Cataloging-in-Publication Data

Schreck, Mary Kim.
  You've got to reach them to teach them : hard facts about the soft skills of student engagement / Mary Kim Schreck.
      p. cm.
  Includes bibliographical references and index.
  ISBN 978-1-935542-05-6 (trade paper) -- ISBN 978-1-935542-06-3 (library ed.)
  1. Motivation in education. 2. Teacher-student relationships. I. Title.
  LB1065.S375 2011
  370.15'4--dc22
                                    2010037980

Solution Tree
Jeffrey C. Jones, CEO & President

Solution Tree Press
President: Douglas M. Rife
Publisher: Robert D. Clouse
Vice President of Production: Gretchen Knapp
Managing Production Editor: Caroline Wise
Senior Production Editor: Lesley Bolton
Proofreader: David Eisnitz
Text Designer: Amy Shock
Cover Designer: Orlando Angel

Acknowledgments

Like any writer, I am grateful to those who listened constantly to my endless prattle about the ideas and viewpoints within each section of the book while it was in the evolutionary stages. How patient my friends and family have been! I am more than grateful to Douglas M. Rife, who held my literary hand from the book's inception to its completion—to Douglas, I am sincerely indebted. His vision, faith, wisdom, and gentle strength can carry any project to its manifestation.

Dr. Bonnie Davis not only served as a sounding board for this book, she also contributed chapter 8, "Cultural Awareness." Bonnie is the essential literary midwife; she urged me to take up my pen and write and has done the same for others as well. Bonnie has always shown a selfless enthusiasm and appreciation for the work and successes of others—a remarkable quality in its own right. Her broad knowledge and sharp insight have been invaluable resources.

A grateful nod goes to the administration, staff, and student body of North East High School in Kansas City, Missouri. They provided me with the opportunity to serve as a consultant and coach during the winter and spring of 2009, and encouraged me to use my experiences as the material for an active research study of the essence of student engagement.

Solution Tree Press would like to thank the following reviewers:

Elizabeth Craft
Teacher, English Department
Sheridan Junior High School
Sheridan, Wyoming

Mark Janda
Teacher, History Department
The Harker School
San José, California

Jackie Jones
Teacher Specialist, Department of
Curriculum and Assessment
Kyrene School District #28
Tempe, Arizona

Lindsey Krawchuk
M. Ed. Graduate, Department of
Educational Psychology
University of Alberta
Edmonton, Alberta, Canada

Dr. Candice Stefanou
Associate Professor, Education
Department
Bucknell University
Lewisburg, Pennsylvania

Visit **go.solution-tree.com/instruction** to download the reproducibles and access live links to the websites in this book.

Table of Contents

About the Author

Mary Kim Schreck serves as an education consultant for districts across North America as well as for the National Writing Project and the National Education Association. Mary Kim also works as a cadre member for Dr. Bonnie Davis's Educating for Change. She has published a professional development book, *Transformers: Creative Teachers for the 21st Century* (2009), and four books of poetry. She has served as editor of *Missouri Teachers Write* and written articles for several education journals.

During her thirty-six years as a classroom teacher, Mary Kim taught in a variety of settings. She taught at an all-girls private academy, a small 270-student rural school that served grades 6 through 12, and a public school of over 4,000 students in three grades on a split-shift schedule. She also spent years tutoring for the St. Louis (Missouri) Special School District. She later taught classes at Brown's Business College and served as a literacy coach at Vashon High School, an inner-city school in St. Louis. Most of her teaching career was spent in the Francis Howell School District in St. Charles County, Missouri, a rural school district that was forced to transform into a suburban district within a few years.

Mary Kim has taught hundreds of teachers through various workshops, presentations, and consulting opportunities. She has been an instructor for the Literacy Academies, a partnership program between the Missouri National Writing Project and the Missouri state department of education, and for the Beginning Teachers Assistance Program offered through the Missouri National Education Association.

Mary Kim lives with her husband, Bernard, at the Lake of the Ozarks in Missouri.

Engagement

Engagement is a hot topic these days among educators at all levels and in all disciplines—and for a good reason. We in education have worked diligently to rebuild standards, curricula, and assessment tools to provide excellence and achievement. With the wonders of modern technology, we have been able to measure, group, and disaggregate data; spotlight skills that were lacking at specific grade levels; and even point the electronic finger at teachers whose students weren't performing or progressing as well as expected. Now we're faced with the one variable that can turn all this effort into ash: the students.

Even when the standards, scope, and sequence seem logical and rigorous, there is no guarantee of success unless the students cooperate and participate in their own education. The students must buy in to the need to follow the carefully tagged, labeled, and filed guides and manuals. So, slowly the eyes of the education community are turning toward what makes a student do what the educator has decided the student must do. That's why engagement has gained hot-topic status. How do we best engage and motivate our students so that all the work we have done has a chance of bearing high-stakes fruit?

Engagement exists in the realm of feeling and contact. This terrain is much different than that of the world of response to data, formulated interchanges, or facts stripped of meaning. You can't *will* or force another person to be engaged, and your motives for engaging your students need to be purer than a desire for higher scores on standardized tests, or those young eyes will see through you immediately!

Teachers and curriculum creators are discovering that a logical presentation of information alone—although very appealing to the adult brain—doesn't stimulate or entice young learners enough to keep them interested and involved (Caine & Caine, 2001). There is more to learning than logic. We are dealing not with little machines but rather with living organisms that react to the world, each other, and the classroom with diverse emotions, minds, bodies, backgrounds, agendas, and needs.

Engagement is a necessary part of the complexity of learning, and there are many concrete actions a teacher can take to successfully engage his or her students. Some of these actions have their roots in human biology research, especially brain research of the last fifteen to twenty years.

The more we know about how the brain functions, the better our choices when deciding on what strategies and interactions to use with our students. For example, studies have verified that emotions are contagious (Goleman, 1991). If a teacher is excited about a topic or lesson, then the students' brains pick up that feeling and react with excitement as well. If a teacher shows distaste for the material in any manner, the students reflect that emotion and believe they have a free pass to not participate or put forth any effort. A teacher who walks into the classroom and announces, "You are lucky you came to school today. You are going to love what we're going to do!" is constructing an emotional state of upbeat anticipation.

With all this in mind, I invite you to learn how to recognize what engages students and brings out their best. I invite you to consider what shifts you can make to create an environment in which students feel confident and safe enough to take risks, make mistakes, and immerse themselves in stimulating learning experiences. Above all, you can bring authentic joy for learning into your classroom.

Each chapter of this book is divided into three segments. "Notes From the Field" illustrates the chapter's topic in a real-life frame through mediums such as journal entries, vignettes, and student comments. "The Discussion" provides a closer look at the topic, including research and the topic's importance and relevance in the classroom. "Steps Toward Solutions" offers practical strategies for implementing the discussed ideas in the classroom.

Woven throughout these chapters are opportunities for reflection. When people say that John Dewey, one of the foremost early education reformers and philosophers, was a proponent of *doing* as the most natural path to learning, they are only half right. Dewey also emphasized that doing without reflection is ineffective. Unless we turn concepts into knowledge that we can accept as our own, they don't stick with us, much less change us. You will be encouraged to mull over the topic—how you feel about the issue—before the discussion and research have their say. This activity serves to prime the intellectual pump and gives the discussion section a deeper richness and validity. After the chapter has paraded its wares across the pages, a final reflection opportunity is provided, allowing you to compare your thoughts with those discussed and encouraging you to choose an idea to try out in your own classroom. Writing down a goal for action cements that idea in your brain and boosts the chances for its implementation.

Chapter 1 focuses on relationships. For many students today, engagement doesn't exist if there is no relationship with the teacher. Where, when, what, and how much we speak with students are all part of the relationship mechanism that sets the groundwork for student engagement. Although verbal exchanges are indeed important, most of the teacher-student relationship is built on the perceptions a student derives from a teacher's nonverbal and often unconscious messages.

Closely tied to relationships are emotions, which comprise the focus of chapter 2. Emotions and the energy they produce are contagious; students pick up and reflect the emotional state the teacher projects. Planning lessons without taking into account the emotional content available is dismissing a large component in the success or failure of that lesson. Emotional literacy is important. Understanding the role of emotions in daily life can help children develop the ability to infer meaning in literature and enrich their writing.

Chapter 3 discusses the necessity and fundamentals of an enriched environment. The eleven key elements of an enriched environment articulated by Marian Diamond, one of the foremost experts in this area, form the base for this discussion. Creating a safe environment and building an atmosphere of celebration and pride are highlighted in this chapter.

In chapter 4, we investigate how intrinsic motivation propels student engagement. We also examine the central role that curriculum plays in encouraging or blocking students' ability to engage.

We take a serious look at laughter in chapter 5. Here we examine fun as a component of engagement and explore our attitudes toward fun and learning. The intense engagement students experience while playing video games and the relationship between fun and productivity in the workplace are highlighted and discussed in relation to the classroom.

Students can't have fun if they don't feel confident. Therefore, chapter 6 explores the teacher's role in building student confidence. A lack of confidence begins a domino effect of negative attitudes and consequent behaviors that make engagement all but impossible. Equally damaging is the teacher's lack of confidence in his or her ability to motivate, challenge, and even manage students. This chapter discusses ways to build confidence for better engagement.

Chapter 7 focuses on changing attitudes, especially in regard to how students perceive their own learning abilities. By helping students change their understanding about the brain—its being an alive, growing muscle instead of a static, set capacity—we can instill in them a sense of empowerment and place their learning within their grasp. If we follow up on this concept by breaking down and translating material into smaller chunks, we can convince even the slowest learners that mastery is possible.

A good follow-up to this change in attitudes is a conversation about some of the more hidden and unreliable attitudes concerning students' cultures.

Bonnie Davis, author of such books as *How to Teach Students Who Don't Look Like You*, *How to Coach Teachers Who Don't Think Like You*, and *The Biracial and Multiracial Student Experience*, is the guest contributor for chapter 8, "Cultural Awareness." As the diversity of student populations grows, it is imperative that teachers have an understanding of the nature of engagement in order to be responsive to the varied cultures represented in the classroom. This chapter provides a look into such a classroom through the lens of cultural relevance.

Chapter 9 spotlights teacher expectations as having a tremendous influence on a teacher's behavior as well as on his or her ability to demand intellectual rigor from the students. This chapter continues the conversation by pointing out that we may sometimes set expectations based on what we see through our personal cultural lenses.

Chapter 10 opens up a metaphorical toolbox of strategies that will produce a student response to learning that leads to academic achievement. In this chapter, we learn how to use both physical tools, such as cameras and technology, and abstract tools, such as lesson-formatting choices and formative assessments, to create meaning for the students.

The toolbox doesn't provide enough room, however, for one of the most important tools: creativity. Therefore, chapter 11 is devoted solely to this engagement tool and 21st century learning requirement. Here we peel back misconceptions about the nature of creativity and discuss how it can be tapped by both teachers and students, how students perceive its existence in their school experiences, and how we can redefine creativity to better embed opportunities for it in our teaching.

Finally, in chapter 12, we take a look at how our current thinking will create our future reality. We discuss what has been reliable in the past and should be taken along with us into the future, and we join the conversation on what qualities an effective teacher must possess. These qualities, the soft skills of teaching, lead teachers to make decisions based on wisdom.

Each of these chapters references a soft skill. In this book, the term *hard skills* is used to describe observable, measurable skills, procedures, knowledge of facts and data, something easily taught and defined—also easily tested. *Soft skills*, on the other hand, are personality or character skills, often called people skills. They are more intangible and are not easily measured, directly taught, or quantifiable. They embrace behaviors such as communicating, problem solving, providing support, listening, maintaining a positive attitude and sense of humor, and so forth. Teachers must learn the soft skills of engagement before they can expect to reach and teach their students.

Relationships

A central theme in Bel Kaufman's novel *Up the Down Staircase* (1965)—as timely today as it was years ago—is that the human encounter between teacher and student is often a more powerful teaching tool than the academic content, the grade, the data analysis, and the hours spent picking apart the curriculum for discrete facts that must be mastered. In this first chapter, our goal is to value and respect that human encounter. Before we can reach, and, in turn, teach, our students, we must first develop a viable relationship with them.

First Thoughts on Relationships

This chapter addresses the quality of your relationship with students as being an outgrowth of your ability to communicate. What kinds of small talk do you use with your students? What is the usual substance of your noncontent communications? How do you perceive your body language and other forms of communication with your students?

2020 thoughts/goals

- open
- approachable
- caring
- inquisitive
- honest
- mental/emotional check
- well-being check

Notes From the Field

The following are a few journal entries from my consulting experience in an inner-city high school. They cover areas of relationship building that are fundamental to producing an educational environment conducive to prompting student engagement and a consequential increase in motivation and achievement.

> Today, Desiree gave me a folder filled with everything she'd ever written, lots of memoir pieces written with such honesty—daddy loves the first daughter best (or so she surmises)—and pages of religious songs. I copied some of the lines I loved so I could read them back to her. I told her to write in a notebook every day like I do and that I'll bring her a notebook when I come back.

> Andrew was a moody boy who often had his head on his desk with the hood of his sweatshirt up, refusing to participate. A week or so ago, he stopped me during class to ask if I knew what a dirge was and then again to find out what a gale was. The young teacher and I answered him. It seems Andrew loves words. Today, he was in one of his unresponsive moods and almost at the point of being removed from class. I went up to his desk and asked him if he was the boy who asked me what words meant a couple of weeks ago. He looked up and answered yes. I exclaimed that he was a bona fide wordsmith and that this was a wonderful and rare trait these days. I told him I loved his word-collecting habit and that I was heading to my car to get him a small notebook so he could jot down words to try to stump me the next time I see him. In fact, I'm going to keep a similar notebook myself and try to trip him up!

> I think my job as a coach is not so much giving teachers lessons as it is showing them how to play out lessons, how to respond to what the kids do, how to adjust and build on what they say. That's more important than the concrete pages of text we cover or strategies we use; it's more the art than the recipe of how to teach.

> Some teachers don't see my small talk with students as being part of the process. They overlook my movement around the classroom, my use of eye contact, my constant attempts at close proximity, and my gentleness in bringing students back to task. Some don't see how easy it is for students to misinterpret the cues they send. They don't realize that their body language can communicate disinterest and a lack of effort. Still others don't see how humor is capable of easing tensions and winning over reluctant learners. All of these are elements that contribute to the student-teacher relationship.

Relationship building is a vital part of my lessons for teachers. I've watched teachers deliver some of my suggested activities for student engagement without that ingredient, and they only work half as well. The affective domain is the life spark of the classroom. Most teachers just need to see how their natural empathy and concern can play out in bettering their instruction. They need to consider how their body language and movement speak volumes to these students.

The Discussion

Years ago, Anne Lamott (1995) wrote a book titled *Bird by Bird* about the inner and outer trials of a writer's life. She tells a story of her older brother, who, when he was ten, had a report on birds to turn in the next morning. He had been given three months to do the project but never got around to starting it:

> He was at the kitchen table close to tears, surrounded by binder paper and pencils and unopened books on birds, immobilized by the hugeness of the task ahead. Then my father sat down beside him, put his arm around my brother's shoulder, and said, "Bird by bird, buddy. Just take it bird by bird." (p. 19)

That advice has carried many through difficult times in their lives, whether it concerned writing, teaching, raising a family, or just meeting the obligations of everyday life. It universally addresses the fear that can paralyze a person when confronted with the immensity of a challenge that lies ahead.

Many teachers are so overwhelmed by the demands and expectations placed upon their shoulders that at times they feel powerless and cave in to a helplessness much like that of their equally overwhelmed students. Often someone will ask, "How is it even possible—with so much to do, to prepare, to cover in a day's time—to begin to build a genuinely individual relationship with each student?" The answer will always be, "Bird by bird." One child at a time, one opportunity at a time.

The Heart of Differentiation

The first two journal entries highlighted two little birds, Desiree and Andrew. I gave each a notebook—Desiree's was a writing journal, and Andrew's was a pocket-size spiral notebook. You might argue, "I can't start giving students things because the others would expect me to give them a notebook or a journal, too, and I don't have that kind of money!" No, not everyone will expect that. Students understand that there is a place for individuality and the recognition of the uniqueness of each student's abilities and needs. It's highly unlikely that all your students will approach you with a folder spilling private writings everywhere as Desiree did. And Andrew? Finding a person so interested in the sound, the weight, and the richness of words is not common. Move through your days responding to what each little bird has to offer or needs by way of individual attention, and in doing so, genuine relationships are cemented. This is the real heart of differentiation.

Relationship building often doesn't require objects, of course. For example, while speaking with a teacher about how easy it is to miss opportunities for showing a little concern or interest, I saw a student walking down the hall toward us who had not been in school for most of the week. I pointed out that we had a decision to make: we could show our agitation at how much class time he had missed, or we could show him how glad we were to finally see him again. I turned to the teacher and said, "Let's experiment! Let's try option two." We showed concern for his absence, asked what was wrong, and told him we had wished he had been here the other day when we did an interesting activity we knew he would have loved. Then we started class. When the teacher asked for volunteers to participate in an activity, guess who had his hand up! And that hand-up attitude remained throughout the entire class period. After class, the teacher said she was surprised that such a small thing as a few sentences of interest had altered his behavior so dramatically. We forget how powerful our words, our attention, and our interest can be. It's often an accumulation of small exchanges that begin to forge the strong bonds of relationships. Tiny gestures of goodwill, of humor, of agreement, and of respect and genuine admiration build and strengthen relationships.

The Positive Effects of Relationships

Engagement is heightened exponentially when a positive student-teacher relationship is fostered and visible in the classroom. A teacher's unbiased, unrestricted, visibly available stance is a dynamic force that will be emulated. For years, I've watched this magic manifest itself in my classroom. I focused on those students who would traditionally be considered untalented, awkward, socially immature, troublemakers, or bully magnets and slowly gave them the attention and respect that is often lavished on the so-called good students or sports heroes. My classroom became a breeding ground for empathy. This occurs because students are fundamentally pleasers and want to stay in the teacher's good graces. What the teacher values, they value. Whoever the teacher "likes" they, too, like, or at least tolerate. Empathy is in our bones. For example, infants will cry at the tape-recorded sound of other infants crying but not at a recording of their own cries (Hanson, 2007). If a teacher is an agent of empathy in a room, it is mirrored by the students. When we bring each other up to our best behavior, learning is maximized.

Learning is also enhanced when students feel connected to the school. A study by the U.S. Centers for Disease Control and Prevention (2009) of more than 36,000 seventh- to twelfth-grade students found that school connectedness was the strongest factor for both boys and girls in preventing substance abuse, sex, violence, and absenteeism. It was the second most important factor, after family, in helping students avoid suicide, emotional distress, and eating disorders. The term *school connectedness* as used here is defined as "the belief by students that adults and peers in the school care about their learning as well as about them as individuals" (Centers for Disease Control and Prevention, 2009, p. 3).

If connectedness is important to you, it will be important to your students. The time and effort you put into developing relationships with your students will exhibit this importance. Fred Jones (2000), who is best known for developing the nonadversarial management procedures Positive Classroom Discipline and Positive Classroom Instruction, reminds us, "Students can always tell what is important just by watching you" (p. 121).

Building Stronger Relationships With Small Talk

In the third journal entry, in addition to highlighting the use of proximity, eye contact, and body language, an educational coach wants her teachers to see the importance of what happens in the room during those small pockets of time between the stages of a lesson's delivery—when the small talk occurs.

The following is taken from a case study written by Regina Gleason and used with permission. A teacher at Margaret Buerkle Middle School in Missouri, Gleason was a participant in the Missouri Humanities Program 2006–2007, sponsored by the International Education Consortium, a program of the Cooperating School Districts Staff Development Division. During the program, the participants were given the challenge of identifying an area of teaching that would benefit from the kind of close scrutiny that an active research protocol could provide. The area that Gleason chose dealt specifically with the relationships she felt were not being naturally formed between herself and her students. Her goal was not only to uncover the cause of the lack of positive relationships, but also to devise a plan to actively change the relationships that were unacceptable to her. In her case study, Gleason (2007) gives a concrete example of how a teacher can use encounters with students to foster an environment more conducive to real academic growth and shows the importance and power of small talk in changing relationships:

> Every year that I have taught eighth grade, my students and I have gone through a cycle of behavior. At the beginning of the year, I have to be a disciplinarian. Most of my students don't care for me

very much because of the discipline I impose in the class environ-ment. I usually don't mind the less popular status because I am aware of the outcomes. . . . After three months of learning what to expect in my class, they know what to do. By the time the semes-ter changes and during the entire second semester, my students and I have a great time in class. I can laugh and smile a lot easier, and so can they. They have begun to see the method of my mad-ness, and I really have a great time as a teacher. Unfortunately this year, it did not happen. The transformation of the classroom was totally nonexistent. I was at a complete loss as to why this year, my students still didn't seem to understand what the expectations were in my class. I continually had to explain simple processes to my students. I seemed to have very little connection with the majority of my students. This is highly unusual.

I decided the best way to increase my connection and relation-ship with my students was to increase the number of positive exchanges with them. To do this, I decided to keep track of the conversations I had with my students throughout each day.

I chose five students from each class. I selected these students because I was concerned about my interaction with these students the most. Some of the students were off task often. Because of their behavior, our communication consisted mostly of my correct-ing them or explaining to them the negative consequences of their actions. I chose these students so that we would have more posi-tive exchanges to balance the frequent negative conversations. The next kind of student I chose was the student that I didn't know very well. I felt that I needed to talk to them so that they wouldn't slip through the cracks. I wanted to be sure to develop a relationship with my quieter students. I found that, in the past, our interactions were limited because of the attention I had to give to students who were either off task or needed special attention with academics.

I developed a checklist for myself to keep track of the interactions I had with these students each day. On the checklist were each stu-dent's name, the day, and a space for the conversation we had. I did include some notes about what the outcomes of some of the conversations had been as well. The conversations were simple. I usually didn't have much time, so I made sure I greeted or saluted each student. On most occasions I was able to successfully engage them in small exchanges. The short conversations ranged from weather comments to success at school, to the kinds of gum we chewed. I continued to keep track of the conversations I had with each student for three weeks. It was not easy to reach every kid that I had chosen, but I was able to casually engage each student in simple conversations throughout a three-week period. Following is a sample week of contact with Student One:

Day One: Told student she did very well and was responsible.

Day Two: Talked to her about staying out of trouble because she could do better.

Day Three: [Discussed] research paper and why it's important to turn in.

Day Four: Congratulated her on her initiative and her work completion.

Day Five: Told her about locker change.

Comments: Throughout the week, student's attitude became better.

Eventually, I began to see a change in my classroom. As I began conversations with one of my key students, I was able to talk to others as well. Where one student was available, several students were there as well. I couldn't just talk to one without the others. This happened time and time again. I would approach one of my target students in class or the hall and other students would join in the conversation. They would join in very willingly, in fact. I was very pleased with the contact I had with all of my students.

I found that not only had my students changed, but I changed. My attitude was better. For example, my journal writing inspired a more positive attitude in myself. After reading it, I realized that I really liked my students a lot more than I was conscious of. This new insight made me see past the negative behaviors of my students and focus on the positive.

Since I set the tone for the entire class, the classes became better. I felt good approaching my students. I made them smile with small talk and they made me smile. I began to look forward to my students and they seemed to feel the same way. During a very short period (three weeks) my students and I felt much better about each other. After a while, the students began to approach me with conversations. Students that I hadn't otherwise had much contact with began to approach me. During passing time, I was in the hall doing hall duty and I looked out of a nearby window. As I was looking out, one of my chosen students came to the window and stood next to me. He looked out of the window and began to ask about the weather. Even though I had been making conversation with him, this was the first time this student approached me with a conversation.

The students, who were usually off task, did change their behavior. Now when they are off task, they either correct themselves without my direction or I only need to give them very little direction for them to focus their attention on their studies. With this group of students, I have more positive exchanges than I have negative, corrective conversations. With all of the students that I chose that had behavior issues, I have definitely seen a change in their behavior. Although some of them do still have issues, most of the students that I chose for the study have very few, if any, behavior problems now.

The quiet students that I didn't have much contact with now approach me more often. I see them in the hall and they start conversations with me. In one class, I have a student that was diagnosed with depression. He was selected as one of my students for the project because he was very good at flying under the radar, he was very quiet, and I rarely spoke with him. I would go days without having contact with him. After I had approached him several times with short conversations, I was out in the hall doing hall duty and as he was approaching the classroom, he exclaimed, "How you doing, Ms. Gleason?" I was so shocked that I gasped before I was able to respond to him.

In the end, my class changed more because I changed. When my attitude changed, then my students' did as well. Here's what resulted from the study:

- I feel much better as a teacher.
- My good attitude sets the tone in the class, and improves the students' attitudes.
- I see more smiles. I give more smiles.
- It's better to be more conscious of your attitude.
- The students and I laugh more.
- My classes run more smoothly. I don't have to correct inappropriate behaviors as much.
- As I increased positive interactions with the students I chose to focus on for the study, my positive interactions with other students increased as well.
- A small action resulted in a significant positive environmental change in my classes. (pp. 74–75)

The Importance of Body Language

Another key factor in building relationships is the use of body language. Paul Ekman (2003), one of the pioneers in this field, explains that what we display on the surface is a direct reflection of what is going on deep inside our brains. Body language is the communication that is transmitted through facial expressions, tonality, posture, use of space, gestures, and other physical responses. Simply put, body language is communication without words. Even so, body language registers just as powerfully in the brain as words, thoughts, and the information flowing from the senses, though it usually occurs on a subconscious level. Nonverbal communication has been estimated to account for anywhere from 60 percent to 90 percent of information transmitted between people (Walsh, 2005). It is only logical that when language skills are limited, nonverbal skills carry more weight. For students in poverty, for students living in dangerous surroundings, and for students from particular cultures, body language is their first language—their natural language of survival (Payne, 2005).

A teacher's sensitivity to students' body language can mean the difference between earning their respect and cooperation and fighting for their attention. The ability to read gestures and expressions makes it easier to respond with far more authenticity, making communication and relationship building more effective. Like any skill, sensitivity to body language can be learned.

For all teachers, a working knowledge of students' nonverbal communication is just as important as knowledge of their verbal communication, and is sometimes even more significant. Patrick Miller (2005), in his article "Body Language in the Classroom," explains:

> The most effective communication occurs when verbal and nonverbal messages are in sync, creating communication synergy. There are some important reasons why nonverbal communication is used: (1) Words have limitations; (2) Nonverbal signals are powerful; (3) Nonverbal messages are likely to be more genuine; (4) Nonverbal signals can express feelings too disturbing to state; and (5) A separate communication channel is necessary to help send complex messages. (p. 29)

Students are aware of the congruence or lack of congruence between verbal and nonverbal messages sent out by teachers almost at once. A study conducted by Vicky Zygouris-Coe at the University of Florida found that "students often interpret things such as their teachers' body language, the order in which they are called on, and the intensity with which they are listened to as signs of their teachers' feelings toward them" (Harmel, 1999). In this same vein, Jim Doud, a former president of the National Association of Elementary School Principals, observed that students find nonverbal clues more realistic than verbal clues and that they are more likely to achieve when they think that their teachers believe they can achieve (Harmel, 1999).

Zygouris-Coe recommends that positive nonverbal feedback—such as "making eye contact, paying attention when students speak and letting them know that you understand their strengths and weaknesses—can make all the difference in the world in removing barriers to the learning process" (as quoted in Harmel, 1999). Since the backbone of relationship building is communication, it would be beneficial for us to acknowledge that a sensitivity to body language is one of the strong and necessary soft skills that is within our reach to acquire.

Proximity, Your Golden Circle

Much of the success or failure in building relationships comes down to a matter of proximity—how physically close or far away we stand from our students. In the elementary classrooms, proximity is a given. Teachers must move around the room constantly, frequently making personal contact with each child simply because younger children demand it. Those who don't—those students who are too shy to draw the teacher's attention—need that proximity even more than the others. In the classrooms of middle and high schools, students sit in their seats longer, eliminating the need for a teacher to patrol them. Some teachers take advantage of this freedom from constant vigilance and spend time at their computers while students work quietly at their desks. This is a mistake. How and where a teacher moves within the room heavily impacts the teacher's ability to manage student behavior, facilitate student learning, and build relationships with his or her students.

Fred Jones (2000) divides teacher-student proximity into three zones. The most influential is the red zone, which extends out eight feet from the teacher. The second, the yellow zone, is six feet farther, making that fourteen feet from the teacher. After that, Jones designates the rest of the room as being in the green zone. His research reports that approximately 80 percent of classroom disruptions occur in the green zone. Jones believes that teachers often underestimate the importance of proximity not only in the effectiveness of classroom management, but also in areas such as relationship building, timely feedback, attentiveness, and lesson momentum.

The personal space maintained between a teacher and a student can also influence feelings of acceptance or rejection. Students who are within the red zone feel a connection with the teacher that allows them to be more comfortable with participating in class, asking questions, volunteering, and taking risks. The farther a student is from the circle of teacher energy, the more fragmentary the feeling of responsibility to pay attention or put effort into class activities.

No matter how often a teacher might invite students to ask questions or indicate when they need assistance, those outside the red and yellow zones of proximity will seldom accept that invitation. However, if a teacher is standing close to a student who lacks confidence or is struggling with an assignment, that student is far more likely to ask for—and get—timely, necessary help. Proximity is a powerful tool for building a stress-free environment that provides the personalized attention and affective and cognitive support that so many students need. For the teacher who wants to begin strengthening relationships with individual students, an awareness of proximity is an excellent place to start.

The Relationship Factor

If all the aspects of engagement—creativity, confidence, emotion, motivation, environment, and so forth—were considered the petals of a lovely water lily, the water that the lily floats upon would be relationships. Without a warm, caring relationship between teacher and student, the other aspects lack energy and effectiveness. Relationships drive the efficacy of the rest of the aspects of engagement and provide a firm foundation.

Steps Toward Solutions

Teaching is much less about what we teach than it is about what students learn. And mostly they learn from watching us—how we think, how we read, how we treat other human beings. For me, engaging students means demonstrating by thought, word, and deed the deep pleasures of a literate life.

—Carol Jago

A good starting point in changing teacher-student relationships is taking the time to observe the relationships that already exist between you and your students. Sometimes teachers can be heard in the lunchroom bemoaning the fact that they don't get along with a particular class and don't look forward to walking into the room and facing that group of students. If you find yourself in a similar situation, make it a point to find out why you feel that way. Surely it isn't the whole class that activates this response. Create a table like table 1.1 (page 16) listing each student's name, and place an X in the box most representative of how you feel when anticipating an interaction with each.

You will soon discover that your feelings of dread are engendered by just a few students, not the whole class. Your emotional response to those few children, however, colors your reactions to the entire class, compounding the problem for everyone.

Table 1.1: Scale of Emotional Responses to Students

Students	Enjoyment	Pleasure	Neutral	Anxiety	Dread
Jason B.				X	
Carissa D.	X				
Drake D.		X			

Try to build or mend your relationships with the students who cause you anxiety or dread. Sometimes this will require separating them from one another. Often when children play off one another, their group persona takes on a life of its own. Speaking with each of these students separately, away from his or her friends, is a good way to break that group-persona mentality. You can then begin to build personal relationships with each individual student.

Also notice who falls into your neutral territory. These students often slip below your radar but would love to be among those who elicit joy when you see them. They simply haven't been able to create that one-on-one relationship with you yet. Building up your relationships with these students can also help turn around your feeling about the entire class.

Create Your Own Case Study

A case study is a great tool for any teacher interested in improving individual relationships with his or her students. By documenting what we really do and say, we bring attention and focus to our behaviors and can then make tiny adjustments that have real potential for changing the dynamic within the entire classroom. Regina Gleason's three weeks of note taking was a small price to pay for the positive relationships that lasted the rest of the year. Why not try out her system and see what your experience is? Read through her case study once more (pages 9–12), and set up your own journal to keep records of contacts with the children you designate as your target students for the study.

Connect Through the Little Things

Try the following exercise to help you connect with your students "bird by bird." Copy your class lists, and paste them in a journal. Next to each student's name, write down the little things you notice about his or her personal traits, strengths, hobbies, interests, and family. Periodically see how much you can fill in about each student. If you have nothing whatsoever to write about some of your students, make it a goal to fill the spaces next to their names.

One way to get information from your students is simply to ask them. However, much will be discovered through observation. It's unlikely Desiree would have claimed to be a writer and Andrew a wordsmith. Those are the kinds of things we need to uncover on our own so we can help them see and appreciate their gifts.

Assess Your Classroom's Connectedness

To assess the connectedness in your classroom, try this suggestion from Fred Jones (2000):

> I used to have teachers hand out a blank seating chart in mid-November and ask the students to fill in the first and last names of everyone in the class. Rarely did the number of correct papers exceed 25 percent. Teachers were typically shocked, but most had to admit that they had invested little time in making it otherwise. (p. 119)

One way to avoid this result is to take a couple of minutes after forming students into groups for an activity and use that time to have students share something about themselves. Give them a prompt to answer, such as: What is your favorite music group? What is your favorite TV series or movie? Do you have a pet? If not, what would you like to have if you could? A short round robin of sharing before the group work begins will ease the tension of having to deal with virtual strangers and make the resulting cooperation in the group more productive. Students will begin looking forward to the icebreaker prompts, will become more familiar with their classmates, and will appreciate how you value this connectivity.

Make Small Talk

Do you make small talk as you navigate the room during class time? A few good opportunities for these quick conversations are:

- Those minutes before class begins in earnest
- While collecting or returning papers
- When rotating from group to group to listen in on the discussions or to monitor progress
- While circulating to check for understanding
- During individual student conferences

Make Eye Contact

Making eye contact is a way to personalize the teacher-student relationship, to signal that you are aware of your students, and to acknowledge their presence with respect. Since shy or timid students rely more heavily on your eye contact to validate their presence in your estimation, make those students who speak the least in your class your eye-contact targets. See if you don't find their body language more receptive toward you and their involvement in class activities more positive. While you're at it, try to pinpoint who gets the lion's share of your eye contact—the bright students? the troublemakers? those in the front rows?

Read Your Own Body Language

We are seldom aware of our body language and how it might be perceived by others. To see what you look like from your students' point of view, watch yourself in action on video. Most digital cameras and cell phones have video-recording capabilities, and many small video cameras, like the Flip, are no longer cost prohibitive. Ask someone to visit your classroom and film you for about ten to fifteen minutes. It's best to do this several times as you will become less aware of the camera and therefore get a more genuine view of how you appear to those in your classroom. No one else needs to see this video; it's for your eyes only.

As you review yourself in action, turn off the sound, and watch your facial expressions. Does your expression change as you respond to each child? Turn the sound back on, and listen for your tone of voice, your volume, and whether or not you sound really interested in student responses. What kind of energy level do you exhibit? Would someone entering your room immediately get the impression that you are passionate about your subject, that you are happy to be teaching?

Play With Proximity and Movement

Since where you stand physically in relation to your students is so important, following are a few suggestions on how to address the issue of proximity in your classroom. When you are in a static position, students tend not to think about you in relation to themselves as much as they do when you are moving—especially if you are moving toward them.

If your students' desks are in traditional rows and you find it difficult to move smoothly among them, have the students in the front row move to the back and have everyone else move up a row. Do this each week; Monday could be Move-It Day! That way, everyone gets a turn in the red zone.

To better visualize what Jones's proximity zones look like, create your own. Gather a rope or piece of twine that reaches from the front to the back of the classroom. Tape a piece of red paper (or tie a scarf) on the rope eight feet from where you will be holding it. The space between your position and the red paper is the red zone. Then measure six feet from the red paper, and tape a yellow piece of paper on the rope at this point. The space between the two papers is your yellow zone. The length of rope beyond the yellow paper is the green zone. Hold the rope and have a student or other teacher hold the other end of the rope and walk with it. If you are at the front of the room, you can easily see just how few students are within optimum proximity (the red zone); you can also see how many are in the green zone, where they feel little relationship to you or your class. Move around the room holding the rope, and see how the different zones of proximity shift when you do. Your job is to see that all students are within your red zone at least a couple times a class to feel engaged.

Since it is important for you to be as close as possible to the largest number of students for the greatest amount of time, your room setup needs to facilitate that proximity as much as possible. Draw a sketch of your room with all the desks and furniture in it. With a colored marker, draw the paths you use to move about the room and from student to student. Are there areas that are difficult to get to? Is your desk in a traditional position at the front of the classroom, taking up quite a lot of your red zone? Draw another sketch of how you could possibly rearrange your room for better and smoother mobility and proximity to your class.

Before making any changes, find out what you really do as opposed to what you think you do. Pick a different class hour every day during one week. Concentrate on how much movement you use during that one hour. Answer the questions on the Classroom Movement Questionnaire (pages 21–22) for each of the five days. What can you deduce from your findings about your movement within the classroom?

Reflection on Relationships

Use the following space to reflect on the ideas in this chapter that you otherwise might not have considered. How will you use the student-teacher relationship to engage and motivate your students?

I never considered that simple proximity could positively or negatively affect student-teacher relations. From personal experience I think small talk with students is super important and beneficial. I want to utilize a student-teacher relationship to create a positive environment to promote engagement.

One new strategy you might try out this week:

Classroom Movement Questionnaire

Questions	Day 1	Day 2	Day 3	Day 4	Day 5	Comments
Did I move to each student's desk at least twice during the class period to say something?						
Was I available for small talk at the beginning of class?						
While students were working quietly, did I circulate and ask how they were doing and check their progress?						
While delivering the lesson, did I move around the room, making eye contact?						
When using an interactive whiteboard or similar technology, did I always stand in one place?						
How long did I sit at my desk?						

Questions	Day 1	Day 2	Day 3	Day 4	Day 5	Comments
Did I sit next to students when they were in groups?						
Did I sit any place other than my teacher's desk?						
Did my students' desk arrangements allow me to move around the room easily?						
Did I speak to and move toward a select few students in the class?						

Emotion

Emotions shape the mood and feel of lesson content, student activities, and the classroom. Emotions also color and solidify the positive or negative attitudes that students take away with them when they leave the classroom. Because emotions are contagious, teachers are able to regulate and utilize the emotions and energy levels of their students for much more effective and memorable learning by regulating and utilizing their own emotions and energy.

First Thoughts on Emotion

This chapter discusses how energy and emotions are interconnected, and the impact of a teacher's emotions on students' feelings about learning. What are your feelings about the role of emotion in your own teaching? What emotions dominate your classroom? Have you ever considered your emotional state to be a contributing factor in the degree of student achievement?

Notes From the Field

The following journal entry covers a class discussion of chapters 14–16 of Mark Twain's novel *The Adventures of Huckleberry Finn*. The purpose of including this class scenario is to highlight the change as well as the range of the students' emotional states within one class period.

Today was "raft day." Earlier in the week, we read that Huck and Jim had found the raft that would serve as transportation for them down the Mississippi. On that day, I marked off the raft's dimensions—twelve feet by sixteen feet—with wide blue masking tape on the classroom floor. We took note of whose desks were in the raft and whose desks were in the river—resulting in a standing joke about those students who had to keep treading water the entire class period.

But today we moved the desks outside of the raft and all crowded into the raft, sitting on the floor. (Students had been warned about this the day before and asked to wear clothes that would be more conducive to sitting than skirts or dresses would be.) Today's chapters, 14–16, contained the heart of the book—both Huck's conflict and choice between his real conscience and his artificial conscience formed by a society condoning slavery, and Huck's awareness and acknowledgment of Jim as an intelligent, good, caring human being. Because the subject matter is so important to the understanding of the book itself, I constructed changes in our normal class procedures to accentuate and heighten the students' emotional responses. I had them in the raft for this reason.

As I read excerpts from chapter 14, we laughed at the exchanges between Huck and Jim over King Solomon and his wives. We laughed at Jim's naiveté and innocent logic. As I read the next chapter, we watched Jim and Huck get separated in the fog all night and, the next morning, heard Huck make up the crazy story about how Jim simply dreamed the whole thing. Then we dipped into Jim's pain-filled heart and heard him chastise Huck for having made a fool of him with his lies while he was so terribly worried about Huck's life the whole night. Huck felt ashamed and apologized. The class moved from laughter to empathy for Jim to a painful recognition of the relationship these two forged despite the social restrictions and attitudes of the day. We saw Huck turn his back on his learned ideas of right and wrong and go with his heart, his emotions. The class discussion was thoughtful, even sobering, as the connections to our own times and the conflicts of conscience that are felt in today's society were shared and expressed.

Closing our books on this note, I announced that it was time for their homemade rafts to take their maiden voyages! They had been assigned the task of making a small replica of the raft that would be able to float for at least ten seconds. This was a sink-or-swim rubric! Using a plastic box filled with water as our Mississippi, each student displayed his or her raft and placed it on the water. Most floated, a few capsized, and a few simply sank. Emotions changed once more from the seriousness of the earlier discussion to laughter and amusement.

On a far different note, the following are two of my favorite student comments that were gleaned from exit slips. In these cases, they are responses to my presence in the class. Both refer to energy as a powerful force in aiding the learning process.

"I appreciate your eye shadow. You're so alive. You're like a teenager in a middle-aged woman's body. Your eye shadow is the exit point of your energy. All your energy is inside of you EXPLODING through your eccentric eye shadow. I appreciate that."

—Greg, eleventh grade

"Overall, I really learned a lot by having you in the classroom. You made assignments interesting and fun. If you want to know what makes kids want to learn, the answer is you—your vibe and presence in the room."

—Samantha, tenth grade

The Discussion

Energy and emotion in our teaching are qualities that we can nurture and call upon to enliven our classes throughout our entire careers. The two student comments were made at the start and end of a teaching career that spanned over forty years. We usually associate energy and emotion with young, idealistic new teachers, but these qualities are just as important for veteran educators to possess and express. Effective teachers infuse their classrooms with the current of life and electricity that is the very substance of emotions. They know that "emotions are a motivating force because they not only order people's subjective experiences, they also energize their responses and give these responses direction" (Turner & Stets, 2005, p. 11).

Most of us have been brought up in the philosophical cradle of Western thought; we have come to see emotion and cognition as separate and distinct as the two sides of the magnificent Grand Canyon. We can trace this great divide back to the ramifications of René Descartes' dualism—the view of the body simply as a machine unaffected by the workings of the mind. Because of this persistent concept, many view cognition and emotion, as Israel Scheffler (1991), professor of education and philosophy at Harvard University, puts it, as being "hostile worlds apart. Cognition is sober inspection; it is the scientist's calm apprehension of fact after fact in his relentless pursuit of Truth. Emotion, on the other hand, is commotion—an unruly inner turbulence fatal to such pursuit but finding its own constructive outlets in aesthetic experience and moral or religious commitment" (p. 1). Yet here is the fuel for the engine that runs the engagement capabilities of our students, the fuel that helps them persevere and stay with us through rigorous material.

Brain research has proved that emotions interact with reason to support or inhibit learning (Goleman, 2005; Jensen, 2003). Part of a teacher's job is ensuring that student emotions support learning. Educators must take seriously the fact that how a student *feels* about a learning situation will determine how much attention and effort that child will expend.

Emotional Energy and Cognition

Samantha's comment about my "vibe and presence" describes emotional energy in teenager speak. Jonathan Turner and Jan Stets (2005), two of the leading voices in the field of sociology of emotions, consider emotional energy to be the sum of feelings and sentiments that rise up in people in specific situations. They explain that people are willing to put out emotional energy if they believe that they will get a positive payback and feeling in return. If this happens, they are willing to exert this emotional energy the next time they are in the same or similar situation. Our bodies resonate with memories of all kinds, especially of situations in which our emotions have been excited. Applying this theory to the classroom, students will return to your class with the expectation of getting recharged if you exert positive emotional energy in your teaching. If students feel they gain both emotionally and intellectually from their experience in your classroom, they will put out their own emotional energy to match yours. If, on the other hand, they have continual negative experiences in your class, they will shut down and be more difficult to rouse from what we often term their bad attitude (Turner & Stets, 2005).

Scheffler (1991) defines an emotion as "specifically cognitive if it rests upon a supposition of a cognitive sort . . . in the service of critical inquiry" (p. 4), for example, or "relating to beliefs, predictions, expectations" (p. 9). He explains that "emotion without cognition is blind, and . . . cognition without emotion is vacuous" (p. 4). The idea that emotions should be separated from rigorous cognitive learning simply doesn't hold true.

The research of Candace Pert (2006) shows that our brains, glands, and immune systems are in constant communication through the molecules of emotion, and knowledge is taken in through our entire being—our bodies as well as our minds. We don't learn simply with our brains. All of our learning is influenced by how we are feeling at the time. Those who think they can turn off their emotions and simply apply a logical, reasonable approach to what they take into their minds are fooling themselves. <u>Learning is an emotional event impacted by one's emotional state</u> (Pert, 2006).

Neuroscientist Joseph LeDoux (1994) explains that emotions create meaning, focus our attention, and control their own memory paths. Our emotional and logical abilities are linked and dependent on each other for optimum functioning, especially in the classroom. Eric Jensen (1998), author of books on the relevancy of brain research to educational practices, suggests that it is worthwhile for teachers to organize their planning around emotions directly.

Today's research is in stark opposition to the mindset that has colored both our thinking and our actions for more than three centuries—the separation of emotion and cognition. "It is possible today to prove in a petri dish how memories live, are stored, and are able to be accessed in various locations throughout the body" in what Pert describes as molecules of emotion (Pert, 2006, p. 218). Teachers must consider how their presentation and their very presence affect the workings of cognitive emotions within their students' bodies for optimum engagement. For example, the pacing and order of activities on "raft day" were geared to initiate emotional responses and increase engagement.

Contagious Emotions

<u>Many studies show the relationship between a teacher's emotional output and a student's level of motivation and engageme</u>nt. When a teacher's enjoyment and enthusiasm are apparent, positive emotions envelop the students and create a mirrored reaction in them that in turn tends to reenergize the teacher—a ripple effect of emotional contagion (Barsade, 2002; Mottel & Beebe, 2000). Daniel Goleman (1995), a leading thinker in the field of emotional intelligence, tells us that "we transmit and catch moods from each other in what amounts to a subterranean economy of the psyche in which some encounters are toxic, some nourishing. . . . We catch feelings from one another as though they [were] some kind of social virus." He adds that "invariably the mood of the one who [is] most expressive of emotions [is] transferred to the more passive partner" (pp. 114–115). For example, a disruptive student who has the most expressive emotions in the room tends to influence those around him or her. <u>The highest degree of emotional content does not always belong to the teacher.</u>

What does this mean for educators? How does this help explain why some teachers seem to get students to work harder, produce better quality, and do so with more enthusiasm than others? One area to examine is the beginning of class. Think about the habitual situations that work together to form how you feel at the beginning of class. Also think of what has occurred during the few minutes before class officially begins—while you are outside your door doing hall duty, getting worksheets copied or materials sorted, or perhaps coming from a before-school staff meeting. Let's take a look at two scenarios with very different outcomes based on your emotional state.

As the warning bell rings, you stand outside your door, urging students to hurry to class, reminding them to pull up their pants or put on their IDs or take off their hats or tuck in their shirts—any or all of the specific school mandates that gradually and subtly become repetitive phrasing and focus. For many teachers, these ingrained reprimands outstrip their ability to see anything about a child except whether he or she is conforming to the rules.

You follow a few students into your room, close the door, and point out infractions. To what is your emotional weather vane pointing? Frustration? Anger? Irritation? Is the tone of your voice mirroring your emotion? You turn to begin class. It is virtually impossible to change to an upbeat, enthusiastic frame of mind and voice immediately. So you have unconsciously set a tone for the class that registers pretty low on the emotional thermometer. Students slouch in their desks. Some already have their heads down. Few, if any, seem to be acting on your request for their attention; many are still talking to their neighbors. No one makes eye contact with you. You raise your voice, reprimand individual students, and, since you get no volunteers to hand out books and papers, begin the lesson in an angry mood. In your efforts to secure good cooperation with school regulations, you have sabotaged your ability to get the most from your teaching efforts.

"But," you argue, "the rules are the rules!" Yes, but I have seen teachers bring students in line with all the rules without destroying their emotional equilibrium—and that of the rest of the class as well. Let's turn back the clock and see how we can perform a do-over of that negative experience. This time, you hold off on addressing the infractions and begin by enthusiastically welcoming the students and preparing them for the day's topic. You call students by name and ask if anyone likes compliments. When two hands go up, you ask those students to hold the pile of books and papers to be distributed and stand at the front of the room. You instruct the remaining students to stand up and get a book and paper from one of the students at the front. You tell them that they can't be given the materials unless they give the student holding the books and papers a compliment. As students go to the front and offer their compliments, laughter erupts in a matter of moments. As everyone begins working, you go to the child with the hat on, the hoodie up, or the ID missing and, in a low, nonconfrontational voice, ask for compliance. The emotional temperature is in the positive range for everyone, and you have addressed the infraction without giving up the entire room to negativity.

"But I'm not the bubbly, jump-up-and-down, emotion-spewing type by nature. Do you mean that in order to engage students, I have to turn into some TV quiz-show moron or stand-up comedian? There's no way!" No, that's not what I mean at all. Teachers can exhibit a very subtle degree of emotional intensity in their classrooms, and still the students pick up on it. The students are well aware of those tiny smile lines around the eyes when the teacher is pleased. They also know what a hint of a frown means.

Movement and Creativity Stimulate Positive Emotions

As we look to scientific findings to help us understand how best to teach our students, we should be looking with dismay at the way districts and schools are systematically dismantling all those segments of the education structure that focus on the needs of the whole child's growth. In an effort to boost test scores, some districts are dropping recess time, physical education, art, drama, and music, cutting time for activities that include movement, socialization, and themed learning in order to incorporate more drill with an emphasis on discrete academic skills. Often these activities and areas of study boost the positive emotions of children and produce the energy necessary to tackle the more difficult work later on in the day. Much has been written on the need for physical movement and creative expression to stimulate emotional well-being and the ability to learn core subjects. While we focus on our goal of educating children for tomorrow, we must acknowledge the impact of emotions on cognitive development and ability to learn, and we must build our action plans around this reality.

Consciously Changing Emotional States

The fourth rule in John Medina's (2009) book *Brain Rules* is that the brain simply doesn't pay attention to anything that is boring. Information devoid of emotional packaging often comes off as simply boring to students. We must constantly incorporate that emotional packaging into our lessons, providing a reason for students to pay attention.

Attention, which is driven by emotion, drives learning (Wolfe, 2001). According to Medina (2009), "When the brain detects an emotionally charged event, the amygdala releases dopamine into the system. Because dopamine greatly aids memory and information processing, you could say [it's like a] Post-it note [that] reads 'Remember this!'" (p. 81). Effective teachers know that regulating the emotional pitch of the classroom is as important as regulating the flow of content, the timing of segments, and the choice of strategies.

I am not aware of an available college course titled "Emotions in Education 101." So how are we to know that we are using emotions effectively in our classrooms? For most of us, it boils down to instinct. You may already be using emotions without even realizing it.

Researchers say that changing the emotional states in a class often can serve to loosen up and invigorate those children who have fallen into a repetitive, nonresponsive attitude (Jensen, 2003). Jensen calls emotional states *action states* that prepare the learner to act in a particular way. Because we are social beings who react positively to person-to-person contact, changing the classroom pattern from quiet seatwork to interactive social networking can immediately affect the action state of the class. The teacher's choice of activities, strategies, and use of timing greatly impacts the emotional state of the students.

Teachers are better able to set up learning conditions when they consciously act to ignite and shift these states. Both cognition and actions are shaped by emotions. By orchestrating these emotions, teachers can provide the students with better access to their cognitive functions and help them remain attentive.

So how can we change students' emotional states quickly and effectively? Physical movement and hands-on activities are surefire methods of igniting motivational brain chemicals (Jensen, 2003). Highly motivating state-changing activities that can be embedded into a teaching system include predetermined and rehearsed gestures to be used by both teacher and students consistently to physically and visually cement the material along with oral repetition of key concepts and procedures. For example, while teaching commas to ninth-graders, I asked the students to make a comma in the air every time one was needed in a sentence that a student read aloud. We would not only make a comma gesture in the air, we would say the word *comma* together as well. If teachers consciously embed movement into their delivery of material, students' attention and interest remain positive and expectant.

The ability to influence students' emotions is one of your most powerful tools and is accessed with the calibration of your own emotions—your voice, your body language, your movement. Like it or not, you have much in common with character actors. When you are in front of twenty-five or so faces, you are on stage and in a role. Each class is another showing of a fine play that deserves your best performance. An actress on Broadway doesn't go out onto the stage and inform the audience that she is in a bad mood and that they shouldn't expect much from the performance. No, she tucks her bad mood away with her makeup case and plays the part with enthusiasm and energy. We need the professional discipline to do the same thing for our students.

Necessity of Emotional Support

During an informal conversation with an education coach, a young high school math teacher was in tears over her inability to motivate her students. After a while, it came through that she saw herself as a "get it done" person who never needed any push, support, or emotional backing to do her work, and she couldn't understand why her students would expect her to supply emotional support. She kept saying that it just wasn't in her personality to provide emotional support and that it shouldn't be necessary. Yet she was in tears at her inability to get her students interested in the subject matter. She seemed unable to buy in to the reality of how important the emotional environment is to the self-motivation of the students—how the teacher who builds the emotional tone in a class succeeds, and the teacher who doesn't has poorer engagement, classroom management issues, and measurably lower results from the students.

Emotion as a motivating factor in the classroom has not been the focus of study for very long. In fact, the only emotion that had been widely studied until the early 2000s was test anxiety. In "Emotions in Education," a special issue of *Educational Psychologist* (2002), six studies reinforce the need for teachers to provide a positive affective climate if students are to avoid negative emotional responses to the class and abandon self-handicapping and avoidance strategies. This positive affective climate manifests itself in what researchers call *emotional support*.

One of the studies, "Discovering Emotion in Classroom Motivation Research" (Meyer & Turner, 2002), reports that with all other things being equal between two teachers—"both teachers appeared to cognitively scaffold understanding and provide opportunities for student autonomy effectively"—the teachers' "patterns of affective support differed remarkably. In the classroom with higher student self-reports of negative affect and self-handicapping, the frequency of positive teacher responses was lower and the frequency of negative responses was higher" (p. 111).

This study, a reflection upon the research on motivation that had been conducted over a ten-year period, goes on to explore what kind of emotional support helps students to activate self-motivation and increase their engagement in the material. Some of these teacher supports include "an emphasis on errors as a natural part of learning, the modeling of enthusiasm and interest in [the subject], and opportunities for student autonomy" (Meyer & Turner, 2002, p. 110). Other common characteristics among teachers who were providing emotional support were revealed: a high degree of overall enthusiasm, a tendency toward seeing humor, and an obvious love of learning. Teachers who are able to give explicit responses, share personal positive emotions with their students, and exhibit their own motivation as learners seem to be key in raising the students' personal emotional responses to the class in general and the subject matter in particular. This combination of teacher behaviors results in higher student achievement. The connection between emotion and motivation is so strong that it seems impossible to study student motivation without considering the impact of the emotional context within which it exists (Meyer & Turner, 2002).

Teaching Emotional Literacy

It's important to make the distinction between emotions that everyone has from birth and those that are learned with age and experience. The only states that are hardwired into the brain are the six primary emotions of joy, fear, anger, disgust, surprise, and sadness. All the others—and there are thousands of emotional states a person can experience—need to be learned (Jensen, 1998; Huitt, 2001). And if they need to be learned, that means they need to be taught.

I've found that one of the main causes of student behavioral problems in class is a lack of knowledge or understanding of how to express emotions that are considered important to the good workings of a group. A reprimand from the teacher usually follows inappropriate responses such as blurting out an answer, talking back to the teacher in a harsh tone of voice, or laughing at others' mistakes. Jensen (2009) reminds us that there is a difference between a child who decides not to act/respond appropriately and one who doesn't realize how to act/respond appropriately (by expressing emotions such as humility, forgiveness, empathy, optimism, compassion, sympathy, patience, shame, cooperation, or gratitude). Instead of receiving a reprimand or worse, such students need to be taught these emotions. Teachers who have always had these emotions in their personal repertoire may find it difficult to imagine students without them and may read inappropriate responses as "attitude," possibly sparking a conflict. Jensen (2009) says that teachers—especially those dealing with children coming from backgrounds of chronic poverty—would do better to teach the proper emotional responses instead.

Much has been widely publicized about the positive effects of adding an overlay of character education to the regular classroom material and how the change in the culture of a school is one of the most positive results of such a focus. Nancy Carlsson-Paige's (2001) essay "Nurturing Meaningful Connections With Young Children" offers these goals for teachers who want to work on emotional literacy with students:

- Help children identify their feelings.

- Help children learn to "read" the feelings of others.
- Help children learn to express their feelings; help them develop a repertoire of words for feelings.
- Help children develop empathy for how others feel.
- Help children connect feelings to the actions and words that caused them.
- Help children separate feelings from action, to learn to think before acting. (p. 31)

Formal education should begin with the cultivation of children's emotional and social abilities rather than with those skills usually connected to the classroom: rational thinking and abstract reasoning. These will come more easily if the child has an awareness of and ability to express feelings and manage his or her emotions (Ardagh, 2005).

This holds true for older students as well as young ones. Studying the literacy of emotions with middle through high school students provides a multitude of unexpected rewards. For instance, focusing on emotions to get to the meaning in texts can add a taste of the new or novel to the basic meat of close-reading exercises. This focus yields a higher degree of comprehension and offers students a method of arriving at comprehension that is completely within their control. This approach not only activates creativity, it also activates an emotional response in the student as he or she pays attention and examines with curiosity that which is different from the norm, the routine. Robert Sylwester's often repeated statement "Emotion drives attention, and attention drives learning" certainly proves true in this respect (quoted in Wolfe, 2001, p. 86).

Another boost to engagement is that the topic of emotions is so meaningful to students—it's about them! Students love to learn how their bodies, their minds, and their brains operate. They can bring up prior knowledge from their own experiences when talking about these parts of themselves—especially when talking about emotions. This prior knowledge base gives the students the confidence to take a stab at interpreting the text since the entryway is one they are personally familiar with. We can use emotions to create a comfort zone in which to investigate those elements of literature that historically discourage the poor readers in our classes and cause them to shut down and give up any effort, such as archaic language and sentence structure. Because moving through the back door of emotional literacy proves to be such a potent and accessible method of presenting abstract and sometimes difficult content to children, there are several lessons and suggestions on this topic in the solutions section for your experimentation.

Steps Toward Solutions

Realize that you are being emotional in the first place. The earlier you recognize an emotion, the more choice you will have in dealing with it.

—Paul Ekman

The first exercises and strategies in this section are geared toward helping you take a closer look at the day-by-day flow of your emotions and how they impact your effectiveness in the classroom. The latter exercises are meant to help the students familiarize themselves with their own emotions and use this knowledge to advance their reading and writing skills.

Get to Know Your Emotions

This first group of exercises deals primarily with your self-knowledge and behavior. One of the best ways to begin controlling or regulating our emotions is to generate an awareness of what emotions we are experiencing in the first place. Let's stop and consider just what and who cause us to experience a particular emotion.

Chart Your Emotional Triggers

Decide on one emotional area that you want to investigate during the school day (for example, how often or when you feel irritated, what student behaviors trigger your more negative emotional responses, or how you talk to a class when you are happy or really like the material). Make a worksheet like table 2.1 for yourself, and reflect upon when, how often, and toward whom you exhibit this emotion. Do this for one week. It will be beneficial for you to see how often you experience an emotion as well as to recognize what seems to trigger it and how long that feeling stays with you.

Table 2.1: Chart of Emotional Experiences

Emotion	Trigger	Response	Duration

Take Your Emotional Temperature

Using a scale of 1 (negative) to 10 (positive), take your emotional temperature before and after each class period of the day and record it in a chart like table 2.2 following.

Table 2.2: Record of Emotional Intensity by Class Period

Period 1		Period 2		Period 3		Period 4		Period 5	

Diagnose your emotional temperature at the end of the week. Look for hours in the day that you are marking as consistently negative. Do you need to put effort into a more positive appearance at these specific times of the day? Why not have each of your students take their temperatures at the beginning and end of class also? Ask them to share their charts at the end of the week and discuss possible causes for their marks.

View Your Emotions in Action

This activity requires a bit of bravery but will be truly worth it. As mentioned earlier, many small digital cameras these days have the ability to take videos that easily download onto your computer. Other small video cameras such as those sold by Flip are accessible, have great sound and video quality, and are very unobtrusive. Ask a student whom you trust to videotape you in action off and on during a week. Or perhaps have a colleague sit in on your class during his or her prep period and tape you. View the videos to see if you can recognize your range of emotions and whether they are having a positive or negative effect on the class.

Stretch and Expand

If you feel you are unable to exude emotion naturally in the classroom (as the young math teacher seemed to feel), why not try to simply expand the emotions you already display? For instance, if you catch yourself smiling at a student, hold it two or three seconds longer; if you find yourself pleased by a student's performance, show that pleasure and stretch it out.

Develop Students' Emotional Literacy

This section will promote activities and methods to help students better understand and use their own emotional abilities. You will find suggestions on how to develop emotional literacy through strategies that complement the regular curriculum and actually provide a platform for instruction in some of the more difficult concepts and skills—tone, inference, detail in writing, comprehending text. Because the initial focus is on the student's knowledge and use of his or her own emotions, we are tapping in to the most highly motivating and engaging of all subject matters: the student's self. We apply this self-knowledge to the content, creating a bridge for students who seldom see any relation between themselves and the curriculum.

Familiarize Students With Their Emotions

This activity serves to pull prior knowledge of emotions from the students' own experiences. Before reviewing a hard-copy list of emotions, it is beneficial for students to see how many they can list on their own and gather from their peers:

1. Each student makes a list of as many emotions as he or she can think of. (There are over three thousand identified human emotions.)

2. The students share their lists with a partner and add any from the partner's list that they don't have on their own lists.

3. Each pair finds another pair and repeats the process.

4. Now, using the Super List of Emotions (table 2.3 on pages 39–42), the students add at least five more emotions that they recognize to their own lists.

The Super List of Emotions is a perfect vehicle for effective vocabulary work. You can ask the students to copy the emotion words they have never heard of or to cluster words under topics such as "positive," "negative," "happy," "sad," and so forth. Students can use the list later to better describe characters, explaining why the words they have chosen would fit. They can make emotional scales (see page 45), placing words on a line in increasing or decreasing intensity. You can use the list as a vocabulary base and let them play with the words. Word lists provide a vocabulary gold mine of possibilities!

Extend the Emotion-Collecting Activity

To encourage the students to explore emotional literacy further, assign the following:

1. Using the Share Sheet handout (page 44; visit **go.solution-tree .com/instruction** to download the reproducibles in this book), the

students write down three of the emotions they had previously jotted down in any of the sheet's boxes.

2. The students exchange one emotion from their lists for one from another student's list. The process is repeated, each student getting a new emotion each time.

3. After three to four minutes, have them sit down and fill out the remaining blocks from the Super List of Emotions (table 2.3 on pages 39–42).

4. Now have the students circle four or five emotions that they can identify simply by looking at people. What does a person look like when angry? Happy? Sad? What is that person doing?

5. Ask for volunteers (about four) to pantomime experiences that highlight one predominant emotion and have students guess the emotion.

6. Now that students can see from the pantomimes the relationship between the emotion and the consequent body language, have them make the same connections themselves. Ask the students to write, on the back of the Share Sheet, three examples of other emotions and body language using the following prompt:

"I knew that Roberto was _____ because he

_____

_____."

Emphasize that you want them to be descriptive about what he was doing, instead of just writing a single word or short phrase. For example: "I knew Roberto was embarrassed when he got caught cheating because his face got red, he wouldn't look at the teacher, and he hunched down into his chair and didn't say anything when the teacher questioned him." Also, tell them that they can add to the basic prompt sentence if they wish.

7. Allow students to share their best example sentences with their neighbors and then with the whole class.

Discuss the Complexity of Emotional Responses

Hold a class conversation on how we actually go through a series of emotions in response to an event. We don't simply feel one emotion at a time but rather clusters of emotions. For example, let's say someone insults us. We could first experience surprise, then confusion, then embarrassment, then hurt, and finally anger. To say we were only angry would be to reduce our complex responses artificially down to a single one.

The class conversation should then move to what kind of emotional responses a person might choose to display and act on. We all feel emotions, but we don't have to respond to each of them physically. Discussing how people can feel emotions but not allow the emotions to dictate their behavior is crucial for helping children recognize and build control over impulsive behavior.

Following is a sample exercise to accompany this conversation using text from a novel.

1. Using a page of text (you can use any page from material you are teaching that would work for you), ask the students to identify the emotions of the characters involved in the action on the page as well as the physical manifestations of those emotions. For example, following is a paragraph from Paul Langan's (2002) book *The Bully* centering on one of the characters:

    > Rage boiled within Darrell, so much so that tears welled in his eyes, making him look as if he really was crying. He hated himself for being so small and weak that he could be humiliated just a few blocks from his own house and he hated Tyray with every cell in his body. But he felt that if he even tried to hit Tyray, he would be beaten to a bloody pulp, that he might never make it home. (p. 66)

2. Have the students compare what they find in pairs or groups of three, explaining what words signaled what emotions to them.

3. Discuss as a whole class how writers tend to use and explain the emotional feelings of characters and why they do this.

4. Ask students to write a couple of paragraphs about two characters meeting during the school day and include not only what they are talking about but how they are feeling and what their body language is displaying.

5. Have the students exchange papers and find the emotions and their manifestations in the paragraphs.

Add Emotion to Writing Prompts

We often give students writing prompts for narrative versions of the materials we are covering. By adding an emotion component to the prompt, we help students produce more thoughtful and better quality results. Following is such a prompt to be used after students have read the book *Night* by Elie Wiesel.

You are Elie ten years after being freed from the concentration camp, and you are to receive a container with seven items from those days ten years ago. You will begin your paper by explaining how you receive the container, where you are, and what it looks like. Then you will open it, and as you pull out each item, you will write about:

1. *The major emotion it brings out in you*

2. *A description of what the item actually is and looks like*

3. *What event in the book it is connected to—including names, places, as many specifics as possible*

Table 2.3: Super List of Emotions

Abandoned	Alive	Beaten down	Celebrating
Ablaze	Alluring	Bemused	Chagrined
Abominable	Alone	Betrayed	Charmed
Abrasive	Altruistic	Bewildered	Charming
Absorbed	Ambiguous	Bewitched	Chastened
Absurd	Ambitious	Bitter	Cheerful
Abused	Amenable	Blah	Cherished
Abusive	Amorous	Blessed	Cold
Accommodating	Amused	Blissful	Cold-blooded
Acknowledged	Angry	Boiling	Collected
Acquiescent	Anguished	Bored	Comatose
Acrimonious	Animated	Bothered	Comfortable
Admonished	Annoyed	Brave	Compassionate
Adored	Anxious	Breathless	Competitive
Adventurous	Apathetic	Breezy	Complacent
Affected	Appealing	Bright	Composed
Affectionate	Appeasing	Broken	Concerned
Afflicted	Appetizing	Bruised	Confused
Affronted	Appreciated	Buoyant	Congenial
Afraid	Apprehensive	Burdensome	Content
Aggravated	Ardent	Bursting	Cool
Aggressive	Argumentative	Callous	Copasetic
Agitated	Armored	Calm	Coping
Agreeable	Aroused	Captivated	Cordial
Airy	Arrogant	Captivating	Cornered
Awkward	Astounded	Careless	Creative
Alienated	Attentive	Caring	Crucified

Continued →

Crushed	Eager	Fretful	Horrified
Cursed	Earnest	Frigid	Horror-stricken
Cushy	Easy	Frisky	Humorous
Cut down	Ecstatic	Frustrated	Hurt
Dainty	Electric	Full	Hysterical
Defensive	Enchanted	Fuming	Impetuous
Dejected	Endearing	Funny	Imposing
Delectable	Enduring	Furious	Impressed
Delicate	Engaging	Gay	Impressionable
Delighted	Enlivened	Genial	Impulsive
Demure	Enraged	Giggly	Indulged
Depressed	Enraptured	Glad	Indulgent
Desirable	Enthused	Gleeful	Inept
Desired	Enthusiastic	Gloomy	Infelicitous
Desolate	Enticing	Glowing	Inflexible
Despair	Even-tempered	Good	Infuriated
Despondent	Exasperated	Grateful	Insatiable
Devoted	Excited	Gratified	Insensitive
Devoured	Exciting	Grieved	Insouciant
Discomfort	Exultant	Grim	Inspired
Discontented	Fanatical	Griped	Interested
Disgusted	Fascinated	Grounded	Intimidated
Dismal	Fascinating	Gushing	Intrigued
Dispassionate	Fearful	Haggard	Inviting
Displeased	Fervor	Half-hearted	Irrepressible
Disregarded	Fiery	Hardened	Irritated
Disregarding	Flared up	Harsh	Jaunty
Distracted	Flattered	Hearty	Jealous
Distressed	Flushed	Heavy	Jittery
Disturbed	Flustered	Hectic	Jolly
Don't mind	Fluttery	Hilarious	Jovial
Doomed	Foaming at the mouth	Hope	Joy
Droopy		Hopeful	Joyful
Dull	Frantic	Horrific	Jubilant

Languid	Overwrought	Ravished	Sensual
Languish	Pained	Ravishing	Sentimental
Lethargic	Panicked	Ready to burst	Serious
Lighthearted	Paralyzed	Receptive	Shaken
Lively	Passionate	Reckless	Shame
Loathed	Passive	Reconciled	Shielded
Lonely	Patient	Refreshed	Shocked
Long-suffering	Peaceful	Rejected	Shy
Lost	Perky	Rejoicing	Silly
Love	Perplexed	Relish	Simmering
Loved	Perturbed	Repressed	Sincere
Loving	Petrified	Repugnant	Sinking
Lukewarm	Pining	Resentful	Smug
Luxurious	Piquant	Resented	Snug
Mad	Pitied	Resigned	Sober
Manic	Placid	Resistant	Solemn
Meddlesome	Plagued	Restrained	Somber
Melancholy	Pleasant	Restraint	Sore
Melodramatic	Pleasing	Revived	Sorrowful
Merry	Pleasured	Ridiculous	Sour
Mindful	Pressured	Romantic	Sparkling
Mindless	Prey to	Rueful	Spastic
Mirthful	Pride	Safe	Spirited
Miserable	Protected	Satiated	Spry
Moderate	Proud	Satisfied	Stoic
Mopey	Provocative	Scared	Stranded
Mortified	Provoked	Secretive	Stressed
Moved	Quarrelsome	Secure	Stricken
Nervous	Quenched	Sedated	Stung
Nonchalant	Quiet	Seduced	Stunned
Numb	Quivery	Seductive	Subdued
Optimistic	Radiant	Seething	Subjugated
Over the edge	Rash	Selfish	Suffering
Overflowing	Raving	Sensational	Sunny

Continued →

Supportive	Thrilled	Unconcerned	Vulnerable
Surrendering	Tickled	Unconscious	Warm
Susceptible	Tight	Uncontrollable	Warmhearted
Suspended	Tight-lipped	Under pressure	Weary
Sweet	Timid	Undone	Welcomed
Sympathy	Tingly	Unfeeling	Whiny
Taken advantage of	Tolerant	Unhappy	Winsome
Tame	Tormented	Unimpressed	Wistful
Tantalizing	Tortured	Unruffled	Woeful
Tantrumy	Touched	Used	Worked up
Temperate	Tranquil	Vexed	Worried
Tender	Transported	Victim	Wounded
The blues	Trepidation	Victimized	Wretched
Thick-skinned	Troubled	Vivacious	Yearning
Thin-skinned	Twitchy	Volcanic	Yielding
Threatened	Uncomfortable	Voluptuous	Zealous

Source: Adapted with permission by Cullen, 2005 (www.mytherapistnc.org/emotions
.htm).

Reflection on Emotion

In this chapter, we discussed how your emotions are contagious, how they can affect your students, how you can purposefully shape the emotional states in a room, and how to teach your students about emotions by helping them identify emotions in their lives and in their reading. What do you feel is the most interesting or relevant information in this chapter? How will you use emotions to motivate and engage your students?

I think the most relevant information is rooted in the way creativity can positively effect emotion and in turn boost students' ability to learn. This is sooo important with my want to be an art teacher. I also believe emotion has a great ability in art to be a motivator because students can incorporate it into ~~your~~ their art.

One new strategy you might try out this week:

Share Sheet

Playing Emotional Scales

Using the words on the Tone Sheet (page 46), choose and order words according to their intensity: the least intense to the most intense. The topic word is in the center.

HAPPY

_____ | _____

ANGRY

_____ | _____

SAD

_____ | _____

EXPECTANT

_____ | _____

Tone Sheet

Aggravated	Detached	Indignant	Quizzical
Agitated	Disappointed	Inquisitive	Reflective
Amiable	Disbelieving	Insolent	Relaxed
Anxious	Disgruntled	Irritated	Remorseful
Apathetic	Disgusted	Jovial	Resigned
Apologetic	Disinterested	Joyful	Restrained
Appreciative	Disturbed	Jubilant	Romantic
Apprehensive	Dreamy	Judgmental	Sarcastic
Arrogant	Earnest	Lighthearted	Sardonic
Audacious	Ecstatic	Loving	Scornful
Baffled	Elated	Malicious	Sentimental
Belligerent	Embarrassed	Manipulative	Serious
Benevolent	Encouraging	Meditative	Shameful
Bitter	Energetic	Melancholy	Silly
Brave	Enthusiastic	Miserable	Sincere
Callous	Excited	Morose	Sober
Calm	Exuberant	Mournful	Solemn
Candid	Facetious	Nervous	Somber
Caustic	Fearful	Nostalgic	Superficial
Cheerful	Flippant	Obnoxious	Surly
Cold	Forthright	Optimistic	Surprised
Comical	Friendly	Outraged	Sweet
Compassionate	Furious	Paranoid	Sympathetic
Concerned	Giddy	Passionate	Taunting
Condescending	Gloomy	Passive	Teasing
Confident	Grave	Patronizing	Testy
Confused	Harsh	Peaceful	Threatening
Contemplative	Hateful	Persuasive	Unemotional
Contemptuous	Haughty	Pessimistic	Uninterested
Content	Hopeful	Pitiful	Upset
Critical	Hopeless	Playful	Vexed
Cynical	Humble	Pompous	Whimsical
Dejected	Humorous	Pretentious	Wistful
Depressed	Hurtful	Proud	Wry
Despairing	Impassioned	Provocative	Zealous
Desperate	Incredulous	Quarrelsome	

Environment

Building community and controlling the emotional climate are key elements for providing an atmosphere in which confronting challenges, accepting differences, and taking risks are prevalent. In this chapter, we will focus on how to create an enriched environment, on the necessity for providing a climate of safety, and on both the physical space and the cognitive space as a possible oasis of well-being for students.

First Thoughts on Environment

Describe your classroom's environment. Do you think your students would agree with your assessment of the environment you construct for them? If not, what would be the differences of opinion? Can you feel the difference in a class environment just by walking into another teacher's classroom?

_____

_____

_____

_____

_____

_____

_____

_____

_____

_____

Notes From the Field

The following piece is a response to an all-call I made soliciting accounts of engagement from students I've taught and colleagues I've worked with. Melissa, a former student, speaks about an incident that occurred several years ago, highlighting an important element of the classroom environment—providing emotional safety:

> My strongest memory is from my junior year, when we had to write a persuasive speech and give it to the class. I hardly remember what I even wrote about, but was so proud of myself for speaking in front of the class without getting sick! I was obviously not the most comfortable person to speak in front of others, but the irony is I do it every day now!
>
> Even more vivid in my memory though is how impressed I was with my classmates. I remember being proud of being in a class with such intelligent, well-spoken classmates. Especially when Matt had just "outed himself" regarding his homosexuality while giving a speech on homophobia. It felt like the class stopped breathing. Although the bell rang, no one moved. Matt continued speaking with such ease, and we were all so captivated by his bravery to approach such a taboo subject. The bell rang for the next class to begin, and we all just sat and listened.
>
> After you dismissed the class, I remember everyone walked out stunned, but the discussion after was not the expected "high school gossip," but rather admiration for his courage and ability to deliver such a well-given speech. We were impressed he felt safe enough to trust us. I am very proud of the class I came from at FHN 2002, Honors English.
>
> And as for your class as a whole, you always came up with inventive projects, writing from different perspectives than typically done in any high school English class. We were never bored. You sparked our creativity and stretched us further than we thought we could go. For that, I thank you.

The Discussion

Melissa provides a poignant example of an environmental climate that allows a young man to feel safe enough to take a tremendous risk in front of his peers. Taking risks is necessary for people to grow and learn. Most would agree with this, but actually providing an atmosphere where risk taking can occur is not always easy. Before a student can willingly take an academic risk—stand up in front of peers and give a speech, read a written piece, attempt a demonstration, or explain a project—that student must be certain that even if he or she makes a mistake or perhaps fails, the world won't come to an end. Educators are the most influential force when it comes to promoting motivation, engagement, and all the other elements that determine an enriched environment.

Diamond's Enriched Environment

Marian Diamond, one of the world's foremost neuroanatomists and a professor of anatomy in the Department of Integrative Biology at the University of California, Berkeley, is considered an expert in the area of environment and its effect on learning. She is probably best known for her breakthrough experiments in the mid-1960s by which she proved conclusively that the brain can indeed grow when exposed to an enriched environment. In the book *Magic Trees of the Mind*, Diamond and coauthor Janet Hopson (1999) list the following key elements of what an enriched environment in a school setting provides for optimum development:

1. Includes a steady source of positive emotional support
2. Provides a nutritious diet with enough protein, vitamins, minerals, and calories
3. Stimulates all the senses (but not necessarily all at once!)
4. Has an atmosphere free of undue pressure and stress but suffused with a degree of pleasurable intensity
5. Presents a series of novel challenges that are neither too easy nor too difficult for the child at his or her stage of development
6. Allows for social interaction for a significant percentage of activities
7. Promotes the development of a broad range of skills and interests that are mental, physical, aesthetic, social and emotional
8. Gives the child an opportunity to choose many of his or her own activities
9. Gives the child a chance to assess the results of his or her efforts and to modify them
10. Offers an enjoyable atmosphere that promotes exploration and the fun of learning
11. Above all, allows the child to be an active participant rather than a passive observer (pp. 107–108)

One can hold up this list of key elements and easily pull out phrases and ideas that show up again and again in researchers' findings about applying brain research to education, how students learn, or what conditions are necessary to activate student initiative and intrinsic motivation: *positive emotional support*; *stimulation of the senses*; *absence of undue pressure or stress*; *pleasure*; *novel challenges*; *opportunities to use the whole-child range of skills*; *opportunities for choice, personal assessment, and modification*; *fun*; and *active participation*. All of these elements need to be in place for a truly nurturing environment to exist and for cognitive learning to be productive and meaningful—an environment such as Melissa described.

The Necessity of a Safe Environment and Withitness

Safety is a multidimensional word when applied to a school environment. It ushers in thoughts of freedom from bullies cornering frailer students on the playground and from mean girls passing lists of less popular girls' names around, encouraging students to add negative comments for each. It floods some of us with memories of elementary, middle, and even high school, where we might have been teased, pushed, or humiliated by fellow schoolmates. Safety in schools requires teachers and administrators to be savvy in much more than standards and data and lesson plans; they must also be alert to the undertow of human behavior.

The role of protector is fundamental to the success of all the other roles a teacher must take on in this career. It's not enough to stand before a class of students and take attendance, assign work, collect papers, proctor tests, and compute grades. The job demands an intense state of awareness of body language and social interaction throughout the entire class period. Students expect and respect this "withitness" that mindful teachers possess. When it's missing, children feel they are on their own to protect themselves and can often tumble into that fight-or-flight mode of thinking that destroys any ability to participate and use their minds effectively.

Withitness is a term first coined in the 1970s by Jacob Kounin to express not only the ability of teachers to be aware of what is happening throughout the room, but also the ability to anticipate what might happen and act preemptively. In his book *Discipline and Group Management in Classrooms*, Kounin (1970) concluded that what teachers do to prevent problems was the key to successful classroom management, not what they did after problems were evident. He also noted that when a teacher handles a discipline problem with one student, there is a ripple effect; other students who were misbehaving tend to stop and pay attention.

Student teachers who were videotaped in classrooms for the purpose of ascertaining the effect of withitness on student engagement and behavior remarked that the experience helped them see themselves from the students' perspective, notice personal mannerisms that might be annoying, become more aware of which students understood the lesson and which didn't, and become more adept at reflecting on their feet and making flexible changes in their instruction (Snoeyink, 2009).

Positive Emotional Support

Diamond's first indicator of an enriched environment is "a steady source of positive emotional support." That support comes not only from the teacher, but from the rest of the class as well. However, it is the teacher's responsibility to set up the norms and guidelines that give students a clear understanding of what is expected of them and what behaviors simply will not be tolerated.

The classroom environment should be conducive to students sharing work without the fear that other students will make fun of them, be overly critical, or not give them the proper attention when they present their pieces. Creating this environment is an important task and can be achieved by having students rehearse their listening skills; by talking about what positive, supportive body language looks like; and by practicing how to respond when a student presents and asks for feedback.

When the ground rules are carefully articulated and practiced, the path toward an engaged class of students is much smoother. Too often, inexperienced teachers think these behavioral skills will magically appear. Instead of being disappointed and upset when students don't behave the way you expect them to, make sure you teach them up front what types of behavior are expected before anything goes wrong.

Creating an Atmosphere of Celebration

Quite a few elements of Diamond's enriched environment are present when a teacher introduces celebrations into his or her instruction. Specifically, celebrations provide a source of novelty and positive emotional support; they stimulate the senses and allow for social interaction in a significant percentage of activities; and they create an atmosphere free of pressure and stress, filled with pleasurable intensity. In other words, they offer "an enjoyable atmosphere that promotes exploration and the fun of learning." Celebrations better the learning process in a child-friendly manner.

Daniel Kahneman (2010), winner of the Nobel Prize in Economics for his pioneering work in behavior, explains that the most critical part of any experience in regard to our formation of memory is the end of that experience. If the end is painful, then the whole experience is thought of as bad. This is one of the best arguments for ending each unit with a celebration rather than the usual test.

For example, to celebrate the completion of our study of Nathaniel Hawthorne's *The Scarlet Letter*, students were asked to depict one of the themes of the book in any mode or media. The only restriction was that they had to use a method unlike the normal writing or speaking presentation they were used to giving in other classes. They were to stretch, synthesize, and portray the essence of the book in a fresh, untried manner. One student considered little Pearl, the illegitimate daughter of the heroine Hester Prynne, to be, as in Hawthorne's words, the "living embodiment of the scarlet letter." She made an outfit for her little sister that was a replica of the clothing little Pearl wore in the book. She synchronized her presentation with her mother's visit to the school with her four-year-old sister so that she had her "living symbol" actually walk through the door at the exact moment she went to the front of the room. Another student composed a piece of music for each of the four main characters that she felt embodied their personalities and their internal conflicts. She and another class member played the pieces in a flute and clarinet duet. One student made a chess game with handmade pieces depicting the book's characters. In his presentation, he explained why these characters matched the roles of the chess pieces so well. During their formal presentations, students were judged on how well they connected their work to the book's themes, characters, and conflicts, and whether they provided any new insights. Later, many class members commented on how much easier it was to write their final exam essay after having been part of such a dynamic review of the material. Because the final celebrations of the book were so enjoyable, most students ended up thinking that studying this novel was not so bad, and they will associate that good feeling with the novel for years to come!

End-of-study celebrations are a lot of fun. Students might present needlepoint pieces and made-from-scratch cakes, musical portraits of the main characters, or sweatshirts that light up with tiny sewn-on Christmas lights. Presentations could include artworks, films, songs, or games. There could be parodies, paintings, video games, blown-up black-and-white photographs of important scenes—the sky's the limit. You'll find that each year's students try to outdo the previous year's students in creativity and quality. All these projects are usually done outside of classroom time. This ensures that it will be even more of a surprise when they start arriving on the appointed day. No one knows what the others are working on or bringing in.

One important part of closing celebrations is the accompanying reflection paper, or paper on the history of the project. Sometimes the story behind a project is more interesting than the project itself. Often students start with one idea and switch to another again and again. Sometimes students experience terrible difficulties that make the project turn out much less spectacular than they originally had envisioned. These papers expose the thinking processes of the students, and the opportunity to explain what happens along the way is an important and integral part of the learning process. And talk about pieces of writing that display voice—these papers shimmer with individuality and voice!

While closing a unit of study with a celebration provides a positive memory and greater clarity and understanding of the lesson, it is also important to *begin* each new unit or topic with just as much celebration. When introducing new material, make sure that the first impression is pleasant and not dependent on words alone. By always beginning and ending a unit of study with an emotional, positive activity, we find ourselves celebrating our learning over and over again.

Celebrations such as these are not effective or memorable if the teacher has not been able to provide an environment that welcomes variety, personal expression, risk taking, laughter, quality work, and mutual admiration. These qualities create the virtual walls of an enriched classroom environment.

Your Room, Your Castle

We've all heard the saying "Your home is your castle," but since we spend almost as much time in our classrooms as we do our homes, it only seems appropriate to make our classrooms our castles as well. Many of us adore preparing and setting up our rooms for the year. We want the physical atmosphere to reflect our love of the subject matter and our belief in the unbounded possibilities that learning affords. When students walk into our rooms, we want them to be able to breathe freely; to feel safe enough to reveal their quirky, always interesting selves; to see proof of their successes; and to be surrounded by color, promise, and novelty.

I've found that one of the best ways to whet students' curiosity about what we'll be doing during the year is to have my classroom walls covered with twenty-by-thirty or even larger color posters of former students in action. Many discount retail stores have their own photo-processing equipment and can blow up a photo to poster size in less than an hour. A couple of these a year is well worth the money, and over time, this builds an environment of anticipation and promise of engaging class work ahead. Instead of those store-bought posters of cartoon characters spouting figures of speech or properties of elements or math processes, why not have pictures of your students doing this? Many students will recognize older students in the pictures and ask, "When can we do what so-and-so is doing in that poster?" Student work always tops anything else as festive decorations in a classroom.

Some schools have policies concerning taking pictures of students; be sure to note these local parameters. A good suggestion is to include a permission sheet with other materials to be signed by a parent or guardian explaining your desire to take pictures of students in action throughout the school year and how you intend to use those pictures. If you compile a couple video clips of students to show during parent-teacher days or open house, your students' parents will likely be eager to help you with every creative idea you come up with later in the year.

Classroom environments contain more than just the emotional ambiance. They contain the teacher's personality embedded in what he or she brings to decorate the classroom. Keep these guidelines in mind when creating an enlivened environment:

- Don't bring in anything that would break your heart if it were shattered or stolen.

- Don't fill your classroom with so much stuff that it becomes an obstacle course for children to walk through.

- Do make colorful, appealing places for student work to be posted.

- Do make sure that at least a few times a semester, everyone's work is displayed in a nonjudgmental manner—not just the "good pieces."

- The more personalized your things are and their work is, the better.

- Create a classroom trademark, a special icon, or a theme. For example, I had an old school desk, complete with the chair connected by an iron post, a lift-up top, and an inkwell, and painted it bright red. I moved that desk all over the room. Students were allowed to sit in the desk and give reports or read aloud.

Your School, Your Kingdom

Most of the discussion thus far on the environment's role in bolstering student engagement has been focused on the classroom. Let's now take a step back and look at the bigger picture: the school environment. The school's environment is more than the sum of individual classroom environments; it is an entity in itself reflecting the values and philosophies of those who work within its walls. If you were to conduct a student survey of the school's environment, you would likely hear many of the following observations:

- I want to be proud of how our school looks. I don't want to be ashamed when teams from other schools come to our school.

- I like the fact that the principal is always in the halls. The last school I was in, we never even knew what the principal looked like.

- A school should be safe. Nobody should worry about getting hurt.

- I like that we have lots of extracurricular activities to choose from. There's something for everyone.

- We need to have a voice in what happens here. If we think we need to change things, there should be somewhere to go and have our say.

- The teachers all care about us here. No one feels like a stranger for very long.

- I feel respected as a person. I like that.

- The walls have pictures of kids doing things. This school honors more than just sports.

The school administration has the lion's share of the responsibility for projecting an enriched atmosphere, but this can never be done alone. It is only with the input and buy-in of the entire faculty that an overall atmosphere is built and sustained. Suggestions on how this can be achieved are addressed later in this chapter.

Rethink Learning Now, according to its website (http://rethinklearningnow .com), is a campaign supported by a growing coalition of individuals, education advocates, civil rights groups, and philanthropic organizations committed to focusing the country's attention on three core pillars of successful education reform: learning, teaching, and fairness. Sam Chaltain, the organization's founder, invites everyone to "help us paint a shared national picture that describes what powerful learning environments, highly effective teachers, and a fair and equitable public school system actually look like" (Rethink Learning Now, 2009). Jan Resseger (2009) of Cleveland, Ohio, responded to this call and provided the following profile of a "powerful learning environment." Her account attests to the power of an administrator and staff who work at providing an enriched environment for students:

> At Chicago's Harold Washington Elementary School, hallways display artist collections of prints and lithographs. Along the primary wing hallway, "Harold Washington Boulevard," the late Chicago mayor's polished black Cadillac sits parked against a wall mural of a police station, fire station, and the city hall. The old building, not an up-to-date space by any means, is Principal Dr. Sandra

Lewis's canvas for displaying the school's values and painting high expectations.

One stairwell displays framed photographs of every one of the school's families. The "dead" spaces as the old staircases turn up three floors are filled with dioramas; the most memorable a tribute to the black cowboy and filled with a real, though somewhat wrinkled, cactus and a mangy stuffed coyote. A prominent marquee hangs over the entrance of the Margaret Burroughs Performing Arts Theatre, the old-fashioned, two-story auditorium filled with the original 1915 black varnished wood seats screwed to the floor. It is painted pink with life-size panels of black performers lining the walls—Duke Ellington, Aretha Franklin, Andre Watts. Dr. Lewis announces, "Our school's band, orchestra, vocal group, and dance troupe perform here." At monthly assemblies in this same space all students posting perfect attendance enter a lottery for a new bicycle.

Even though control and order are paramount at this school—students walking to the gym or the library in straight rows, students reciting in unison a memorized creed about values, respect, and expectations—Dr. Lewis announces, "At our school we have fun." The working jukebox in the principal's office makes me believe she is right. Sometimes when I'm awake in the night or driving in traffic, my mind wanders to Harold Washington Elementary School. How would I be different if I had been lucky enough to be part of such a place? How will their time at this school shape the lives of the children there? What seems sure to me is that Dr. Lewis knows that to transform the lives of her school's children, she must fill their days with much more than basic reading and math and the drilled down test-prep that is being driven by the federal No Child Left Behind Act. At Harold Washington Elementary School, education is an act of joy.

Although Jan Resseger focuses primarily on the contributions of the principal at Harold Washington Elementary School, it is the combined effort of all the stakeholders in a school that produces an environment in which "education is an act of joy." The amazing externals, such as those described in this piece, would not exist without the teachers' efforts and support. The externals of a school can only give a glimpse into the environment created by each teacher in each class, but that glimpse is definitely one that can foster a momentum of mutual intention as a visible reminder of a school's shared goals.

Steps Toward Solutions

Thinking deeply about what we are doing leads us to ask better questions, break out of fruitless routines, make unexpected connections and experiment with fresh ideas.

—Ron Brandt

The following suggested steps will help you to create an enriched classroom that meets Diamond's standards. We will also move beyond the classroom to take a look at the physical appearance of the school campus.

Revisit Diamond's List

Reread Diamond's list, and determine which elements are your three best—your strengths in providing an enriched environment for students:

1. Includes a steady source of positive emotional support
2. Provides a nutritious diet with enough protein, vitamins, minerals, and calories
3. Stimulates all the senses (but not necessarily all at once!)
4. Has an atmosphere free of undue pressure and stress but suffused with a degree of pleasurable intensity
5. Presents a series of novel challenges that are neither too easy nor too difficult for the child at his or her stage of development
6. Allows for social interaction for a significant percentage of activities
7. Promotes the development of a broad range of skills and interests that are mental, physical, aesthetic, social and emotional
8. Gives the child an opportunity to choose many of his or her own activities
9. Gives the child a chance to assess the results of his or her efforts and to modify them
10. Offers an enjoyable atmosphere that promotes exploration and the fun of learning
11. Above all, allows the child to be an active participant rather than a passive observer (Diamond & Hopson, 1999, pp. 107–108)

We seem to improve more quickly and with more efficacy when we work on our strengths instead of concentrating on our weaknesses. So, write down the ways you consistently provide an enriched environment for your students.

After recognizing yourself at your best, it will be easier to take on another key area to strengthen.

Look at Your Classroom

Draw your classroom or, even better, take a few pictures of your room. Label all the physical areas that mirror an item on Diamond's list (page 57). For example, "Allows for social interaction for a significant percentage of activities" could apply to any place where seating arrangements are flexible and can be easily shifted from whole-group to small-group activities or provide the opportunity for partners to work together. "Gives the child an opportunity to choose many of his or her own activities" can apply to a learning center where children can pick the type of activity they would like to do or places in your room for students to find and choose differentiated work that complements the skill set or information to be mastered. Sometimes seeing what your classroom actually looks like helps you to realize whether or not you have these enriched-environment elements accessible to your students.

Host a New Teacher Shower

Those of you who have taught for more than a couple of years have likely managed to accumulate a wide assortment of materials to fill and enliven your room. Encourage the newest members of the faculty to create their own enriched environments by hosting a "New Teacher Shower" to help them get started.

Appraise Your School Campus

How do you feel about the impression your school as a whole gives students and strangers? Often we get so used to being in a building that we begin to lose our ability to see it from a visitor's eyes. Walk through your building as a visitor would, and jot down what you notice. Mark the items on your list with a 1 to represent those things outside of your control, a 2 to represent those things within your control as a faculty, a 3 to represent those things that are within your personal control to change, or a 4 to represent the great things people are doing to provide a positive appearance.

Make it a point to compliment those people responsible for the 4s. Compliments have a way of increasing the likelihood of an activity because of their reinforcement value. Choose one of the 3s to take on as your next project. The 2s can be brought up at faculty meetings when appropriate. Often a conversation needs to take place before action is taken. Start that conversation. One person can make a powerful difference.

Poll your students on how they feel about their school environment and your class environment in particular. Perhaps together with the students, you can create a poll that can be distributed to other groups of students for their input regarding school environment. Present your findings and suggestions to the administration.

Use Music to Enrich the Environment

Do you use music in your classroom? The following suggestions for implementing music come from Willy Wood (2009) of Open Mind Technologies, Inc.:

- The best times to use feel-good music are the transitions—when students are coming into class, getting materials out or putting them up, transitioning between tasks, and as they are leaving the room. The key to becoming good at using feel-good music is kid-watching. You will be able to tell if they like a song or not by how they react.

- There are literally hundreds of ways you could use music to match the activity in your classroom, to add some fun and laughter into the learning environment. There are songs to match the weather, songs to match the season, holiday songs, songs that match the day of the week . . . and on and on.

- When should you use background music? When your students are doing any kind of quiet seatwork, which could include silent reading, writing, doing worksheets, working math problems, and so forth. The goal here is to put a soft pad of sound over the room in order to cover up irregular environmental sounds such as a student tapping a pencil on a desk or a foot on a chair leg, or a teacher walking down the hall having a conversation on a cell phone.

Of course, when using music in the classroom, it is always important to be sensitive to the effect the chosen music could have on each student. Some students are more easily distracted than others, and it might be better to not add a layer of music to their environment.

Make Up Classroom Celebrations

A book that should be on all teachers' bookshelves is Byrd Baylor's *I'm in Charge of Celebrations*. It provides a fresh look at the little things that can be cause for joy and celebration.

Ask students to help you fill in a Celebration Calendar. Days could be designated for celebrating a new student, a new class pet, math symbols, the library, and so on. Encourage them to be creative and read Baylor's book for inspiration if needed.

Reflection on Environment

Environment is a blend of physical surroundings, emotional tone, and personal comfort. Imagine that you have no restrictions and can create the perfect classroom environment for engagement. Describe it below. Add the elements that really resonated with you and the questions that cropped up while reading this chapter.

_____

_____

_____

_____

_____

_____

_____

_____

_____

_____

_____

_____

_____

_____

_____

One new strategy you might try out this week:

_____

Motivation

Motivation is a key component of engagement. In this chapter, we will take a look at the different types of motivation, what creates motivation, and what can kill motivation. Students might blame the curriculum for their lack of motivation, but teachers realize the curriculum itself cannot be blamed; the teachers must make the curriculum engaging, thus motivating the students to learn.

First Thoughts on Motivation

We often hear teachers complain that their students just aren't motivated. What do you think this means? What are some of the causes for the lack of motivation? What are you currently doing to help motivate your students to learn the material?

_____

_____

_____

_____

_____

_____

_____

_____

_____

_____

Notes From the Field

The following excerpts are from personal journal entries written during a consulting job in an inner-city high school.

Jasmine took home the letter assignment we worked on in class, and she revised it a couple of times. She had it on a disk and couldn't get it to print out on the library computer the day I was in her class. I want a copy of her finished product. Jasmine is an intelligent young lady who is just awakening to the realization of how good she really can be at writing if she plays with it a while. She didn't have to rework the paper; she already got the points for it. She's experiencing that intrinsic need to better her piece because she knows she can, and she wants to! I need to talk to her about this, help her see that what she's doing is so important.

I am at the point where I can conduct a full class and have students paying attention, reacting, participating, listening to my crazy stories, laughing, BONDING, really working . . . students smiling and acting exactly how classes responded when I was a full-time teacher in a predominantly white, upper-middle-class environment. This confirms the fact that these children, many of whom have been given up on, can learn anything anyone else can learn if the expectations are high enough and the teacher knows how to engage them. The teachers are seeing this, too. . . . I'm seeing teachers move away from the front of the room, make small talk instead of yelling at students, urge the students gently to work or explain what's keeping them from working, and put on a more respectful demeanor toward each of them.

Observing one class this afternoon, I was confronted with the problem that comes up when the students are primed, ready, prepared, and eager to be engaged in the class, and the content just isn't accessible. Nothing is more disheartening for everyone involved. When students can't grasp the material, can't make connections, see nothing that makes sense, it's harder on them to be actually ready and willing to learn than to never really put out the effort in the first place. The disappointment is palpable. The frustrated teacher keeps going with a "dead lesson," and her frustration ends up in a tirade of blaming and reprimanding students for not trying. What we teach is as much responsible for fostering or killing engagement as how we teach. Teachers must be encouraged to change gears when the curriculum isn't working—encouraged and shown how and when to embed alternate methods and materials into their teaching.

The Discussion

Jasmine's work on the letter assignment (reported in the first journal entry) is an example of pure intrinsic motivation and reward. She had already received a high grade for her paper; she just wanted to make it better. She was responding to an internal challenge to reach her own level of mastery. According to Richard Ryan and Edward Deci (2000), creators of the self-determination theory, "Perhaps no single phenomenon reflects the positive potential of human nature as much as intrinsic motivation, the inherent tendency to seek out novelty and challenges, to extend and exercise one's capacities, to explore, and to learn" (p. 70).

Because motivation is interlaced with our efforts at educating, there is a great deal of research on the efficacy of one method of motivation over another and of extrinsic versus intrinsic rewards to stimulate student motivation. Ryan and Deci (2000) have found:

> threats, deadlines, directives, pressured evaluations, and imposed goals diminish intrinsic motivation because, like tangible rewards, they conduce toward an external perceived locus of causality. In contrast, choice, acknowledgment of feelings, and opportunities for self-direction were found to enhance intrinsic motivation because they allow people a greater feeling of autonomy. (p. 70)

Such findings seem to fly in the face of the intense pressure on teachers to achieve gains on standardized test scores, or see their personal evaluations suffer.

In his segment "The Surprising Science of Motivation," presented at the TEDGlobal 2009 conference, Daniel Pink reported findings that the carrot-and-stick incentive plans that dominate business practices do little to motivate people in any sort of meaningful fashion. In fact, they blunt real innovative, creative thinking and produce much lower performance than when no incentives, pressuring deadlines, or punishments are imposed. Pink proposes a system that takes advantage of intrinsic motivation. This system is based on three pillars:

- Autonomy: the urge to direct our own lives
- Mastery: the desire to get better and better at something that matters
- Purpose: the yearning to do what we do in the service of something larger than ourselves (Pink, 2009)

Pink's pillars mirror the findings of educational researchers who report that "the more students were externally regulated the less they showed interest, value, and effort toward achievement and the more they tended to disown responsibility for negative outcomes, blaming others such as the teacher" (Ryan & Deci, 2000, p. 73). Students who are "taught with a more controlling approach not only lose initiative but learn less effectively, especially when learning requires conceptual, creative processing" (Ryan & Deci, 2000, p. 71). Studies also show that the "children who had more fully internalized the regulation for positive school-related behaviors were those who felt securely connected to, and cared for by, their parents and teachers" (Ryan & Deci, 2000, p. 73). So, again, the presence of choice, the ability to master the material, and the existence of meaningful relationships and activities seem to be what moves students to find intrinsic satisfaction, motivation, and engagement in their work.

During a walkthrough of a Maryland middle school, I saw children choosing toys and turning in tokens they had earned during the week for doing their schoolwork. The back of the classroom looked like the warehouse for a carnival booth—shelves and shelves of bins containing everything from stuffed animals to little games to jewelry to action figures. This was a display of extrinsic rewards in all their glory.

In the fall, some school districts hold mega lotteries and drawings for televisions, electronic games, and bikes to urge parents to get their children to school on the first days. Some districts are experimenting with paying children for attendance or for achievement on state-mandated tests. Verbal wars rage over the effective value of such practices.

Although extrinsic rewards seem to grab students' attention and provide motivation, this motivation is fleeting at best. If we are aiming for that deeper, long-lasting intrinsic motivation that will carry a child the entire distance of his or her life—the motivation to persevere, to make wise choices, to put off immediate gratification for the benefit of reaching future goals—carnival toys and payoffs aren't going to do the trick.

Balance is needed in this war of words over the efficacies of extrinsic and intrinsic rewards. Both can exist in mutual harmony if a teacher achieves that wise balance.

Many of us have found that what we emphasize is what we get. If our emphasis is on points or grades, then that's where the class conversation will be focused. If our aim is on quality, personal best, and risk taking, the collective gaze of the classroom has to shift away from the linear grade measuring stick and go inward. De-emphasizing grades is not easy, especially with students who have learned to count by adding and comparing the number of stars they accumulated daily as kindergarteners with those of their companions. The "I've got more than you, so I must be better than you" mindset begins early.

Orchestrating Intrinsic Motivational Experiences

At first, Mrs. Triefenbach's outside-of-class right-brained projects were quite an enigma for her students. Contrary to normal assignments, with these, Mrs. Triefenbach was short on concrete directions, long on students' ability to make personal choices, and outrageously short on point value and comparison grading. Students were urged to try something they'd never done before—take a risk, extend themselves—all the while assured that if it didn't work out quite like they expected, it was no big deal; their precious grade points wouldn't bear the scars. And here is the strangest point of this whole nontraditional approach: she got amazingly good quality products, and about 98 percent of students turned projects in.

One especially good set of products came from the Literary Dinner Party event. Students signed up for a name of an author or character they had "met" during the semester. Their job was to prepare a table place setting that would reflect the personality and relevancy of the chosen person, including an appropriate prop, short poem, place mat, dishes, and so forth. One year, Mrs. Triefenbach reserved the library for the dinner party and had each of her over 125 students assemble the place settings in the morning before school began. She invited other teachers' classes to tour the tables and to fill in answer sheets, guessing which ones were which. Although this method was good and caused quite a stir in the school, she concluded that the in-class dinner parties, during which each student had a better opportunity to explain why he or she had chosen the specific pieces of each place setting and had the time to read the poem to the class, were much better. The imagination, creativity, diversity, and novelty inspired all of her students.

With this explained, let's listen in on a conversation that usually cropped up at least once a year between Mrs. Triefenbach and a student.

STUDENT	How come nearly all of us got the same grade?
MRS. T	Because nearly all of you did what I asked you to do.
STUDENT	But some are much better than others.
MRS. T	True.
STUDENT	I really worked hard on mine.
MRS. T	I can tell. Did you like the results?

STUDENT   Yes. I'm really proud of my project.

MRS. T   Would you have put in less time and effort if you knew the overall grade might be pretty much the same?

STUDENT   No. I got this idea and wanted to do my project this way and wouldn't have been satisfied with less.

MRS. T   So what's the problem?

STUDENT   It doesn't seem fair. I mean mine is so much better, yet others got the same grade I did.

MRS. T   Oh, so it's the grade you worked so hard to get, not the finished product?

STUDENT   Well, no. . . . Well, yes. . . . I don't know how I feel about this.

MRS. T   That's the reality of intrinsic/extrinsic rewards. Satisfying yourself is the intrinsic part; getting the grade, the recognition, is the extrinsic part. You actually are experiencing both. You are simply a bit hung up on what others are getting in comparison to you, right? I suggest you get over that; it's not all that important. Stick with exercising that internal satisfaction muscle. That's where the action is if you want to really get something out of this life.

This might sound like it defies everything our school culture is trying to produce—clearly articulated levels of competency, lists of students by order of personal proficiency, and so forth. But in fact, most of her class products provided these, having been guided by state standards with student- and teacher-formulated rubrics reflecting clear expectations and an understanding of what constitutes high-quality work. Some assignments were just more open with minimal guidelines, like the assignment discussed previously, for the specific purpose of teaching the value and experience of working for intrinsic satisfaction—for risk taking with a safety net.

Confronting and Dissecting Boredom

There has been a steady decline in the amount of choice that teachers are allowed when it comes to what can be used and how to teach to the accepted standards, concepts, and skills. While most guides and compiled binders of strategies and lessons still have the word *suggested* in their prefaces and headings, fewer and fewer district and building administrators are willing to allow much deviation from the suggested materials. Motivation is one of the elements sacrificed when this occurs.

Studies indicate that up to two-thirds of public school students are classified as disengaged from learning (Blum, McNeely, & Rinehart, 2002). These students report feelings about school ranging from apathy to anger; they report being bored and frustrated most of the school day. Even though research "links higher levels of engagement in school with improved performance" and "researchers have found student engagement a robust predictor of student achievement" (Klem & Connell, 2004, p. 262), more and more schools are moving toward a uniform curriculum with a singular emphasis on a narrow vein of intellectual achievement that dangerously implies a one-size-fits-all approach to classroom teaching. Differentiated instruction expert Carol Ann Tomlinson (2004) warns that this approach is ineffective for most students and harmful to some and urges a more concerted effort to promote three educational principles that emerge from brain research: emotional safety, appropriate challenges, and self-constructed meaning.

Appropriate challenges and self-constructed meaning are seldom found in prepackaged, "easy" teacher programs. But this isn't the most fundamental reason for broader latitude in teacher choice. A teacher needs to own the lessons, to digest the concepts, objectives, and standards. A teacher needs to make the decisions on how best to pace and present these to his or her particular group of children at a particular time of the school year. Any time a textbook company or program designer advertises the materials as "easy to follow, all decisions made for you," a red flag should instantly appear. If teachers aren't allowed to choose how to teach the curriculum, they don't own it, nor are they engaged in watching it play out in the classroom. This lack of authentic engagement on the part of the teacher is consequently a very real cause for disengagement on the part of the students.

Many educators spend their careers scouring what they read, watch, hear, and notice for interesting material to pique student curiosity and to pull them into lessons. Many teachers are naturally good at delivering lessons and building a safe, student-friendly environment. As important as a teacher's style, personality, sense of humor, natural friendliness, and knowledge of affective domains are, the ability of the teacher to make the necessary choices that allow the curriculum to come to life and create meaning is even more important. Take that away, and you have gutted the job, destroyed the satisfaction of utilizing creative energy, and demoralized the teacher. The lack of student engagement that this creates becomes more and more evident and difficult to change as the child ages.

The 2006 High School Survey of Student Engagement (HSSSE) report *Voices of Students on Engagement* compiled by Ethan Yazzie-Mintz, project director, is a survey of 110 schools from twenty-six different states of the United States that highlights this problem with disengagement. The study reported that two out of three high school students are bored in class at least every day; 17 percent are bored in every class. When asked "If you have been bored in class, why?" 75 percent responded that the material wasn't interesting; 39 percent stated that the material wasn't relevant to them; 32 percent said the work wasn't challenging enough; 31 percent reported no interaction with a teacher; and 27 percent said the work was too difficult. Three out of four students find the material the major reason for their boredom (Yazzie-Mintz, 2007). Yet in spite of the consistent call from educational researchers and major content-area organizations for a wider and more relevant selection of materials to be available to students, the pressure and directives from administrators demand that teachers stick to the text, not veer from the pacing guides, and, in many cases, stick not only to the textbook but to the script.

In response to this dilemma, researchers Richard Strong, Harvey Silver, Matthew Perini, and Greg Tuculescu (2003) state, "Curriculum design based on four natural human interests—the drive toward mastery, the drive to understand, the drive toward self-expression, and the need to relate—will not only reduce student boredom, but will yield boredom's opposite: abiding interest in the content that students need to learn" (p. 24). Most of our curriculum design is geared toward the area of cognition. Neglecting the two areas of self-expression and the need to relate to others accounts for much of the boredom and consequent failure we see in a large part of our student population. The teacher who is allowed the freedom to manipulate the curriculum is able to address these areas when planning specific activities and projects for the class. Most of Marian Diamond's requirements for an enriched, invigorating environment for students support the four natural human interests.

As researchers are finding—and as most teachers already know—there is a higher correlation between student interests and achievement than between achievement and cognitive ability (Strong et al., 2003). When a teacher is not encouraged to find materials and strategies that can make the subject meaningful for the students and instead is simply expected to "just cover it," students tune out. The demanded adherence to expensive packaged programs and prescriptive methods of instruction is often the real culprit in disengaging students today. As the HSSSE survey (Yazzie-Mintz, 2007) reports,

> The current educational environment is shaped by a sharp focus on accountability; in this context, passing rates, graduation percentages, and standardized test scores are the most common

barometers of high school success. But the students who participate in HSSSE are looking for something more in their high school
experience: to be actively involved in their learning, to be intellectually challenged, to be taken seriously as individuals, and to mean
something within their high school communities. (p. 13)

Simply put, students want to be engaged. The teacher has the power to allevi-
ate the problems that students are reporting. By actively involving the students
and building relationships, educators can demonstrate that students are taken
seriously and their voices are heard. Far more is within the teacher's control
than one might think.

Motivation and the Flow Experience

Mihaly Csikszentmihalyi is best known for his work explaining intrinsic motivation through his theory of *flow* experiences. Most of us have experienced a
time when we were so absorbed in what we were doing that we lost all sense
of time and paid little or no attention to anything going on around us. At such
a time, we are giving our full concentration and are completely involved in the
object of our interest. We also feel free from any fear of failure or self-con-
sciousness, and we feel more alert and alive than we do at other times. This is
flow. In this state, the experience is its own reward. This state exists between
too much anxiety on one side and boredom on the other—it is the perfect balance between challenge and skill (Csikszentmihalyi, 2008).

We want the learning we introduce to our students to lead to flow experiences.
We want students lost in the magic moment of a breakthrough in understanding, of the creation of a new solution, or of successfully mastering a challenge.
When students are surprised when the bell rings, take this as one of the highest compliments of your ability to motivate and engage them in your subject
area.

There can be no engagement if the expected learning and efforts at arriving
at that learning are not robust and meaningful to the student. The learning
experiences are at the center, the heart, of the engagement process, where all
the information about effective strategies and rigorous standards comes into
play. This is where attention to multi-intelligences, learning styles, hands-on
activities, meaningful real-life experiences, and the needs of the whole child all
find their place for consideration. Fundamental to the construction of a state
of flow for the students is the teacher's grasp of the content as well as his or
her ability to deliver it. Teachers need to be continual learners in their fields of
concentration. It's virtually impossible to make material interesting if one isn't
familiar with it in the first place.

Teacher Assignments Affect Student Motivation

What a teacher is assigned to teach has a huge impact on the degree of enthusiasm and effectiveness in the classroom throughout the year. All too often teachers work to master new material only to be given an entirely new subject or grade level to teach the following year. Teachers need the opportunity to fine-tune the techniques of a familiar subject matter. Teacher assignment is one area that could improve teacher effectiveness without costing the district a penny but is seldom considered an important focus. Of course, the need to shift teachers with enrollment changes is a reality, but there is too little concern extended to teacher assignment. Matching a teacher's strengths and interests to his or her teaching assignment is a positive factor in increasing students' motivation and engagement.

Although this seems to be an issue primarily in the administrator's arena, it is one that teachers need to consider seriously and bring to the attention of those who make scheduling decisions. Many school administrators poll their teachers at the end of the year to get their input on what area or grade level they would like to be placed in and take this information into account when building schedules. If this isn't the case, perhaps it would be a good agenda item to bring up at a faculty meeting.

There is much talk about how the one-size-fits-all approach to education is detrimental for the student; it is equally detrimental for the teacher. Teachers aren't all alike and can't be plugged into teaching slots indiscriminately without repercussions to the health of the entire school program. Building strong units that scaffold learning and lead to a rigorous grappling with concepts and skills takes time and sustained thought. If a teacher's assignment is constantly changing, there is no time to master the material and manipulate it to the point of building highly effective units that differentiate according to student needs. This subtly undercuts the teacher's ability to grow and teach at peak performance levels and, in the long run, undercuts the entire school's ability to produce large achievement gains.

There is a strong push to tie student achievement to teacher evaluations. For example, an integral part of the scoring for the Race to the Top funding grants is a school's ability to align teacher evaluations more closely to student achievement and hold teachers accountable for a lack in achievement (U.S. Department of Education, 2009).

Often in large inner-city districts, teachers don't know what they will be teaching until a few days before school starts. A few weeks into the school year, far too many find themselves transferred to another assignment or school to balance out class sizes. What a handicap to place upon teachers who will be judged and perhaps even paid on their performance and ability to raise student achievement!

In spite of these and other obstacles that confront each teacher walking into a classroom, the teacher always has the power to motivate and engage his or her students.

A Relevant, Meaningful Curriculum

The third journal entry (page 62) describes a class that was ready to learn but couldn't because of the material. This is not an isolated incident. I don't know anyone who has ever been caught up in a feeling of excitement and desire to learn from an anthology. The nature of most textbooks runs counter to our desire to grapple with problems that need to be solved, questions that need to be answered, quests that need to be taken to arrive at understanding and satisfaction. Because of this reality, teachers must manipulate the material to spark the excitement and curiosity that cause engagement.

The curriculum should reach and resonate within the child; the child shouldn't have to work constantly to find meaning and relevancy in the curriculum, although that is exactly what is being asked of the students in our current archaic structure. Small, discrete skills and pieces of information need to be embedded into larger, more meaningful contexts. They are never satisfying and engaging on their own. Learning definitions and terms outside of a larger context of meaning isn't learning that sticks or is capable of being transposed to other circumstances. The material needs to be a means to an end, not an end in itself. If your students' intrinsic motivation is a goal, a worthwhile exercise is a careful examination of just how meaningful your content delivery is.

Effective teachers recognize when students perceive the lesson as being empty of meaning and significance. Frantically, they work to make changes as soon as they see the confusion, frustration, or lack of interest on students' faces. They don't just keep plowing on, explaining that the material *must* be covered and the students *must* pay attention and learn it. Sometimes a teacher simply stops and, after a few seconds of complete silence, asks the students how the lesson is going. This usually generates responses that the teacher can then address. When it seems there is a lack of understanding, sometimes a teacher cuts down the amount of material he or she had planned to cover and backs up. Some teachers acknowledge that the current content isn't as interesting as everyone would like but explain that it gets better in a little while and if they can just bear with it, all will come together. This acknowledgment of how students are feeling often brings them back and results in their putting more effort into the lesson.

When asked about the relationship between curriculum design and a feeling of accomplishment, a veteran teacher responded:

> The only time I have that deep cellular feeling of harmony with what I am teaching and also have a consequent high level of student engagement is when I am in the middle of a good novel with my students or a good strong thematic or project-based unit. Then the material has complexity, variety, depth, and a good span of activities complementing a demanding understanding of underlying principles of both the frameworks of quality literature and the workings of human nature. Then the material grabs and focuses my students in real learning. This is when I am at peace with my teaching and feel what I am doing holds a tremendous amount of value. I never feel this way when content is sliced and diced and presented piecemeal on a paper plate. To be honest, I really never have students open up their textbooks except to access pieces that are part of a larger whole we are investigating. The textbook is a reference source, not my course; a recipe book, not the plan for the banquet.

Most students surveyed by HSSSE (Yazzie-Mintz, 2009) who gave reasons for their dissatisfaction, despair, and feeling of suffocating boredom in our schools pointed to the curriculum. Most dropouts are saying much the same thing (Yazzie-Mintz, 2009). We seem to have gone backward in our race to ensure student achievement in many important areas that revolve around curriculum. Here are a few such areas that need to be examined and redefined to more adequately meet the needs of the 21st century learner:

- **Teacher empowerment**. Instead of giving teachers packaged products to teach or scripted lessons to read, allow teachers to use their professional expertise in creating new teaching materials and reconstructing older ones as they deem necessary. The pathways to meeting standards should be broad and varied.

- **Team empowerment**. Reconsider the way professional learning communities (PLCs) are being used. Their basic purpose is to build effective learning and raise the level of excellence through group collaboration. PLCs are not meant to be an arm for administrative dictates or a method of communicating administrative mandates more efficiently.

- **Curriculum**. A total transformation of the curriculum is necessary to overhaul what learners need to know and do to thrive in the 21st century. Reinventing curricula, instead of revamping curricula, should be the center of our thinking and conversations. Instead of just copying from the board or from books, learning should be a quest to find answers, to solve problems, and to create.

- **Structure**. Question the need for school buildings as they are constructed now and "seat time" spent like prison sentences. Question the need for expensive textbooks. Consider the possibility of creating learning groups according to interests and aptitudes, after basic functional skills are developed and basic health needs are met. Why not stop grouping by age alone?

While this list may seem like it is geared toward administrators, teachers have the ability to influence school issues. Most curriculum and building decisions are constructed by committees that always include teacher representatives. Standards ask for teacher input at every level. The more responsibility placed upon the teacher to deliver student achievement, the more weight his or her opinions should have.

Motivating Boy Writers

The range of variety in content materials and activities affects the quality of students' active-learning experiences. If this range is narrow and limited, students tend to be immune to any efforts teachers make to engage them in the work. One example that illustrates how this narrowing of opportunity can influence student motivation and engagement is in the area of writing.

Ralph Fletcher, one of the gurus of the writing workshop format, spoke at the Gulf Coast Conference on the Teaching of Writing 2009 in Destin, Florida, on June 30, 2009. He explained how he had stumbled upon an issue that had been privately gnawing away at him as he went from classroom to classroom working with students on their writing: the boys simply hated most of the writing opportunities. As he began to focus on the what and why of this situation, he became aware of how today's education scene tends to narrow the scope of what boys are allowed to write about. He also noted how this narrowing of genre and the list of acceptable topics is resulting in many of our boy writers shutting down. In his keynote as well as in his book *Boy Writers: Reclaiming Their Voices* (2006), Fletcher makes the case that educators need to give boys a little more commonsense leeway. Young boys often would rather write cartoons, fantasy, science fiction, movie scripts, comic books, horror, graphic novels, sports writing, sports commentary, or creative nonfiction than the traditional personal narratives, memory pieces, letters, and prescriptive paragraphs that are the dominant focus in classrooms today.

He also makes the point that boys love action and writing about conflict. One of the fallouts of the Columbine tragedy has been a pervasive feeling of suspicion and disapproval when boys try to write on any topic that contains weapons or superheroes or conflict of any kind. In fact, Fletcher suggests that this backlash of zero tolerance for anything violent could easily be the single most destructive force in stunting the writing growth of elementary-age boys. Boys often prefer to write fiction, yet this is seldom offered as an opportunity in what Fletcher sees as a tightening and scripting of the writer's workshop.

To engage boys in writing, Fletcher urges teachers to widen the circle of what boys are allowed to write about and to realize that unlike the girls in their classes, boys write to please other boys, not the teacher. We should also realize that upper-grade boys would greatly benefit from drawing as part of their composing process. The mix of talking, drawing, and writing is a surefire method of engaging both boys and girls of any age in the process of writing.

What is true here about writing is equally true about reading. Educators need to develop a sensitivity to the reading tastes of boys. One of the best ways to get a young boy to read is to have an adult, preferably a male teacher, suggest a book that he will be sure to like. When a teacher makes a recommendation outside of class work, it sends a message of personal interest. By keeping up with current books and filling up the library shelves, a teacher is equipping him- or herself with a great source for engaging students in outside reading.

Discipline Problem or Motivation Problem?

When focusing on student performance, we need to take a hard look at the causes of student behaviors and students' consequent underachievement. What can look like discipline problems are often problems of motivation instead. Let's say we accept the definition of a discipline problem as offered by James Levin and James Nolan (2002), professors at Pennsylvania State University: "behavior that (1) interferes with the teaching act, (2) interferes with the rights of others to learn, (3) is psychologically or physically unsafe, or (4) destroys property" (p. 4). This would mean that acts such as not paying attention, refusing to do or turn in homework, daydreaming, not participating in a discussion, and not coming to class with necessary materials aren't necessarily discipline problems but rather problems stemming from a lack of motivation. Two of the primary differences between a discipline problem and a problem of motivation are the effects on others and the interventions that are necessary to solve the problem. Motivational problems usually do not block the learning of others in the room; they are usually specific to the individual student. Also, it takes a lot longer to solve a problem of motivation than a problem of discipline. Often teachers treat the behaviors stemming from a lack of motivation as infractions of the rules and dole out punishments when they occur even if they do not meet the qualifications for discipline problems. If this happens, a teacher's later attempts to provide effective interventions to improve a student's motivation are considerably more difficult.

Motivational problems can be due to "low levels of self-confidence, low expectations for success, lack of interest in academics, lost feelings of autonomy, achievement anxieties, or fears of success or failure" (Stipek, 1998, as cited in Levin & Nolan, 2002, p. 5). Children with motivational problems *can* do the work but *don't*. We can't engage and motivate all of our students all the time, but it is our job to recognize and explore the reasons why some seem so reluctant to exert the slightest amount of effort to learn. Punishment and threats aren't a very successful method of turning this behavior around. The first step in helping the unmotivated child make a change for the better is simply to acknowledge that these behaviors are manifestations of a lack of motivation instead of immediately viewing them as disciplinary infractions.

Steps Toward Solutions

> *Teachers should have a really solid grounding in how people learn if they want to succeed in engaging their students in learning.*
>
> —Geoffrey Caine

Since motivation is so deeply related to a child's sense of self-worth and ability, one of the first places to begin in building motivation is at the relationship level. While developing relationships with individual students, a teacher begins to uncover what will motivate each most effectively. The exercises and suggestions that follow address this need to reach the individual student and also examine what we can do for the class as a whole, as well as for ourselves.

Apply Guidelines for Intrinsic Motivation

Gleaned from the current research on extrinsic motivation, here are a few guidelines to think about when considering rewards as motivators:

- Use extrinsic rewards sparingly.
- Provide rewards that are closely related to the task accomplished.
- Only give rewards when they are clearly deserved; otherwise, they become meaningless.
- Start small in the beginning; the school year is long.
- Monitor your students' reactions. Some research demonstrates that using extrinsic rewards lowers achievement and negatively affects student motivation.
- Ask students what would make a good reward; the answers might surprise you.

- When using comments on student work as "rewards," look at the quality of those comments—are you being specific about what is good or just making blanket statements about the overall assignment?

- Consider immediate feedback on student work to be the best motivator.

Choose a couple of these guidelines to focus on when considering your reward procedures.

Contemplate Teacher Assignments

Teacher assignments—the classes teachers will be teaching—are not mentioned in most books on teacher quality and effectiveness except to spotlight the horrible yet still common practice in many schools of placing the least experienced teacher with the most difficult students. As the stakes get higher for teachers to provide student achievement, this area of the school's decision-making process should and will come under scrutiny. Consider the following:

- Who makes the teacher assignments in your school? Is this person familiar with the teachers' strengths and personal interests?

- Is it possible to make an appointment with this person to discuss what your interests are for the following year? If so, make your case for a specific area or grade level.

- You might suggest that the teachers in your school be given the opportunity to write down what they would like to keep or change and begin a procedure for input into the assignment process if none exists at present.

- Teacher assignments could be a good topic for discussion at a faculty meeting. Consider sharing alternative ways that other schools decide a teacher's assignment.

- Does longevity in your school determine who teaches what subjects? Is there a rotating system? Is there a way to challenge the longevity factor that sounds reasonable?

Examine Your Strategies and Procedures

There is wiggle room within each curriculum guide for you to define the strategies and the procedures you are going to use to deliver the material. Reflect on the following questions concerning situations in which the lessons aren't working:

- Do you reflect on how you feel the day's lessons have worked as you drive home or before you go to sleep? Do you make mental notes about how you could improve lessons the next time? Do you act on those ideas?

- Do you impulsively try to blame someone for a lesson that goes flat? The students? The material? The administration? Do you come around to taking responsibility for the success of your teaching? (This is a huge question that warrants your consideration.)

- If the material is too difficult for your students, how do you handle this? Do you break down the concepts into smaller, more easily digestible segments? What do you do if it's too easy for them?

- If you feel the curriculum is too confining and narrow, what steps have you taken to bring this up in your department? What steps have you taken to join a curriculum committee or work with your PLC to create alternatives?

- If your school is using an RTI (response to intervention) model, what assistance is available to help you reframe the material in an effective manner for better understanding?

- Do you take advantage of new ways to deliver your material instead of repeating what you have always done in the past? Sometimes years of familiarity with a curriculum lead to a lack of enthusiasm that students pick up and emulate. Try this suggestion: every summer, designate one or two units to rework, update, and breathe more life into.

Use the RAFT Approach

How do we structure assignments to present material as a means to an end rather than an end in itself? Use the RAFT formula—role, audience, format, topic—to engage and challenge students to shift their perspectives to show and use their knowledge instead of simply regurgitating it to satisfy a grade requirement.

The RAFT formula can be used in nearly every discipline and grade level to frame assignments in an engaging manner. With a RAFT prompt, the point of view is usually that of someone other than the student, and the audience is usually not the teacher. The format is never the ordinary theme assignment format, and the topic is usually connected to the current learning. For example, a RAFT prompt for *The Odyssey* could be: you are Ulysses (role) on your ten-year journey back to Ithaca from Troy. Your task is to write a series of letters (format) to your wife, Penelope (audience), and explain the many adventures you are having and why it is taking you so long to get back (topic).

Here's an example assignment that Katie Salen developed for a sixth-grade Spanish class as it appears in Eric Liu and Scott Noppe-Brandon's (2009) wonderful book *Imagination First*:

> A group of Boobonians have been kicked off their home planet and materialize in a universe where only Spanish is spoken. Your challenge is to help these aliens learn it—and quickly, so that they can survive. Every week they transmit to you an artifact from their new universe: a map, calendar, a weather report, a diagram of the body. You've got to help them make sense of these artifacts in their new tongue. Conveniently, you can converse with them using an interstellar version of Skype. (p. 133)

Pick a topic in your curriculum that can be turned into a quest for information or the means for solving a problem. Use the RAFT as your guide—or should we say, your lifeboat! Make a list of important topics you teach that might be enhanced by requiring a RAFT writing assignment from your students during the year.

Examine Your Assignments

Reading and writing are basic to a child's education, so let's examine the assignments we give our students and figure out how motivating they actually are:

- What kinds of reading and writing experiences do you make available to your students?

- Are these experiences in and of themselves engaging? Explain.

- Do they match the concerns and natural interests of their age group?

- Do your students have the opportunity to choose what they would like to read or write about? How have you set up this opportunity for them?

- Go through your lesson plans, and star the opportunities you offer that allow your students to make choices. No matter how many you count, add more in your next set of lessons.

- Go through your lesson plans again, and see if the type of writing you are asking the students to do is pretty much all the same. Include a variety of formats and genres in your next set of lessons.

Take Action

Following is a list of concrete actions that a teacher can implement to ensure that students are more motivated. Circle one or two that you can most readily add or increase in your teaching:

- Add novelty to your unit introductions.
- Set clear goals for learning and share them with students.
- Give reasons for studying a particular skill or concept that make sense to students.
- Set up game-like and simulation formats.
- Help develop action plans and goals for each student.
- Give immediate and honest feedback.
- Use rubrics that provide clear expectations.
- Provide a variety of sensory experiences, especially visuals.

Reflection on Motivation

Think back to those activities and assignments that truly motivated you as a student or that truly engaged your students. Write them down. What do these assignments have in common? How can those common elements be repeated more often in your instruction?

_____

_____

_____

_____

_____

_____

_____

_____

_____

_____

_____

_____

_____

_____

_____

_____

One new strategy you might try out this week:

_____

Fun

If teachers could spend as much time and energy on ensuring that their students were enjoying their learning as they spend on collecting data, testing, and transmitting information, chances are achievement would increase. Often the problem with low-scoring students isn't that they *can't* do the work, but rather that they *don't want* to do the work. In this chapter, we will look at why we fear the word *fun* and believe it is something to be kept separate from rigorous, high-level learning, and we'll take a hard look at our own attitudes toward the enjoyment of learning.

First Thoughts on Fun

Have you ever envied another teacher's ability to engage a class, to make the learning experience seem so much fun? Do other teachers look with suspicion at those whose classes are considered fun? Where do you fit in? What is your attitude toward fun?

_____

_____

_____

_____

_____

_____

_____

_____

Notes From the Field

I remember my third year as a teacher. Surrounded by cornfields, the school was a small, private, rural school of 270 students in grades 7 through 12. Each teacher taught six classes, and some, like me, taught seven with no prep hour. I taught seventh-grade reading and seventh-grade English back to back, then ninth-grade English, tenth-grade English, twelfth-grade literature, another tenth-grade English, and finally seventh-grade art.

The teacher in the classroom across from mine was older than I was. She had the same students I had, but what was happening in her room wasn't happening in mine. I could hear her class in action, and it sounded like the students didn't have a moment's chance to get into the kind of trouble they caused me. Every minute was filled with something interesting and fun. She was magnificent. I wanted so much to ask her what she was doing that had those students mesmerized. I never heard her raise her voice at one of them. They came bouncing out of her room at the bell with smiling faces. I wanted to ask her for help, but I didn't. I was too embarrassed to ask for help. I was new at this school and was intimidated by the older, more experienced teachers. Instead of realizing that asking for help was a sign of maturity, I thought it showed weakness. The bottom line was that I was too proud.

It took much trial and error before I could teach like that woman. If the school had had a more sharing atmosphere, perhaps I could have cut that time in half. The students would have benefited from the existence of a teachers' mentoring program back then. Those students weren't having much fun in my classes that year. At least I had the good sense to know that what I was or wasn't doing wasn't effective, that the lack of the fun factor did have an impact on how my students were learning.

Who decided that learning should be serious, difficult, quiet, and labeled "work"? When did we decide that fun should be relegated to being an add-on after the real work of learning is over? Does this thinking have its roots in how we view work itself? Do we view work as inherently devoid of enjoyment or fun?

The Discussion

We have an ingrained suspicion of mixing fun and work. *Work* is often the default word for a boring routine. Historically, we can trace our ideas of work back to the Greeks, who assigned all work to slaves. Later, during the Renaissance, the concept of work was uplifted, and the trades were elevated to the level of art. Many became products of the Protestant work ethic promulgated by Calvin and Luther. A distinct shift in the perception of work came next with the separation of craftsmen's physical work and professionals' intellectual work; brain was elevated over brawn. The Industrial Age brought a scientific slant to work, and the unions began their efforts at protecting workers from being looked upon and treated as objects. In the 2000s, the relationship between living and working came into question, and as a product of the Digital Age and its emphasis on innovation, the movement toward merging fun and work became visible (Yerkes, 2007).

Fun is often the default word for interesting, challenging but not overwhelming activities. For many students, *fun* means that time flies, that they never know what will happen next, that they get into the action and forget about being self-conscious, and that they get to talk. But for a number of teachers and administrators, the word *fun* means veering from the curriculum guides, drifting off-task, sacrificing rigor and serious focus on the material, tending toward a lack of control or discipline, and giving in to the students. And below that definition lie thoughts such as "I'm not funny," "Games and gimmicks are a waste of precious time; we could be working on basics," "It takes too much effort or imagination to teach like that," and "They shouldn't need me to entertain them—this is school, not a video game." If a teacher does consider having fun in the classroom, often he or she wonders when the "real" work begins: "What happens when the work isn't fun? How will I get them to do the real work then?"

We need to change our mindsets and understand that work can be fun and fun can be work. All student work—even the real work—should be fun-filled and include challenge, choice, and proper feedback.

Fun and the Business World

The business community has begun to question and explore negative attitudes toward work. Books with titles such as *Managing to Have Fun: How Fun at Work Can Motivate Your Employees, Inspire Your Coworkers, and Boost Your Bottom Line*; *Fun Works: Creating Places Where People Love to Work*; *1001 Ways to Energize Employees*; and *301 Ways to Have Fun at Work* fill bookstore shelves these days. Their theories are well worth noting: when fun exists in a workplace, stress is reduced, absenteeism goes down, and morale is improved. The business community has found that "when fun is integrated with work instead of segmented from work, the resultant fusion creates energy; it cements relationships between co-workers and between workers and the company. When fun is integrated into work, it fosters creativity and results in improved performance" (Yerkes, 2007, p. 8). Substitute *school* for *business*, and this easily applies to the education world as well.

The Fun in Video Games

That teacher I so admired in the opening piece had never heard of a computer or a video game. If she had a television, it only had a couple of channels. Yet she knew what the video-game creators know about engagement and motivation. She knew that children need challenges that are reachable and immediate feedback to know how they are doing, what to change, and what to repeat. She knew they need surprise and novelty to keep the material interesting. They need to feel like winners, not failures. They need to have fun.

At this point, not many schools are seriously considering video games as classroom fare—according to Marc Prensky (2006), less than 1 percent—but those that do use them "applaud games as a way to help develop 21st century skills, such as collaborative problem solving, multitasking, and networking. Some educators compare game play to the scientific method: Players enter a phenomenon that doesn't make sense, observe problems, form hypotheses, and test them while being mindful of cause and effect" (Yusuf, 2008). I'm sure that wonderful teacher would be the first in her school to try out such a teaching tool were she still in the classroom today.

We don't have to change the school into a video-game emporium to reap the engaging benefits of these games. We can look for ways to incorporate video-game formats in specific areas of the learning process that traditionally are devoid of motivation—namely, homework or drill. For instance, while Larry Marsh taught statistics to undergraduates at Notre Dame, he developed an interactive electronic homework system he dubbed "Adventures in Statistics." He explains,

> Adventures provides instant feedback and does not permit incomplete or sloppy homework. Homeworks that are not perfect don't get any credit. Students have to keep trying with reworded questions and new data samples until they get it right. Everyone's ultimately a winner. It's just that some are winners a lot sooner than others. Before each class the teacher can monitor how much time each student is taking in solving each problem. Teachers can then adjust their lectures to address areas of general weakness, but also identify an individual student who is having difficulty with a particular concept to help after class. (Marsh, 2009)

Certainly those interested in building RTI alternate teaching strategies and embedding immediate feedback assessments in those strategies will be taking a long hard look at such efforts, especially at how electronic tools that mimic the strengths of video games can be replicated in every subject area. Katie Salen, an associate professor of design and technology at the Parsons School of Design in New York, adds that "games create a need in kids to figure something out, so the need to learn comes from the kids, not the teacher" (as quoted in Yusuf, 2008). Even though games may be labeled as "fun," they are actually a big step toward intrinsic motivation and steady engagement.

Laughter: The Prescription for a Healthy Classroom

All teachers need to become familiar with the strange things that make children laugh. The humor of a middle-school boy is very different from that of an adult. Understanding what makes that seventh-grade boy laugh hysterically can be a very valuable piece of information. Many a day I heard laughter coming through the walls and flowing under the door of that seasoned teacher's room. She never seemed the funny type when conversing with adults, but she certainly had mastered the art of making children see humor and enjoy belly laughter with her day in and day out.

If you don't understand what makes your students laugh, ask them. Have a "Laugh In" show, and tell everyone to bring in a joke, reference to a movie, cartoon, or whatever makes them laugh. Such an assignment could also act as an icebreaker. It won't take long to find out what a particular age group sees as humorous.

We all have a sense of humor—some more obviously than others—and we all know what it feels like to have a good laugh once in a while. Laughter can work miracles when it comes to setting the tone of a class. It is one of your most effective tools in cutting through stressful situations, winning over hard-to-reach students, and lifting spirits. Laughing is a wonderful way to activate and increase the body's flow of dopamine—the happy chemical.

However, there are a few guidelines for utilizing laughter in the classroom. Never try for laughter that originates in sarcasm. Young teachers who haven't dealt long with young people sometimes aren't aware that the humor they use with their peers isn't applicable with their students. Kids don't get sarcasm. They often feel they are being made fun of by the teacher, and any positive efforts at using humor are destroyed. Never allow laughter at the expense of a student. The only one who is fair game to be the butt of a joke is you. You can tell funny things about yourself whenever you want, but not about others. Laughing at your own mistakes or foibles makes you seem human to your students—one of the most endearing qualities you can aim for.

Laughter is more than just a nice addition to a classroom; it's amazingly powerful in physically improving the damaging effects of stress that block the ability of students to learn and remember. Matt Weinstein, in his book *Managing to Have Fun*, reminds us that people for thousands of years have realized that laughter is good medicine. It's only been since the 1990s, though, that actual medical and scientific research has been able to document that laughter and play have a beneficial effect on physical health—that laughter equals relaxation. Scientists have shown that the body's natural painkillers, endorphins, are released during periods of laughter. When this happens, a natural high takes place that opens the system for pain reduction. Along with this, the body generates T cells that boost the immune system (Weinstein, 1996). A logical consequence of this might just be that if we laugh more often, we will take fewer sick days and decrease the absenteeism of our students. That's a stretch, but who knows, it might just work!

The Fun Environment

An informal survey of students I conducted during the winter of 2009 revealed what young people consider to be a fun classroom. Most responses could easily be translated into what educational researchers are calling effective teaching strategies and a good learning environment. These students didn't think that fun in class was goofing off; rather, they thought of a fun class as one with a high degree of active learning and participation. Here are a few of their thoughts on fun in school:

- "Fun is when we're active and not just listening to the teacher."
- "Fun is doing different things that are exciting."
- "Fun is when we get to talk."
- "Fun is not worrying that we'll get in trouble."
- "Fun is when the time goes by really fast."
- "Fun is when the work isn't too hard or too easy."
- "Fun is when the teacher isn't yelling at us."
- "Fun is drawing or having music on or playing games."
- "Fun isn't like normal classes with worksheets and hard tests."
- "Fun is working together and not always by myself."
- "Fun helps me remember what we learned in class."
- "Fun is when I can try new things and not worry about getting things wrong."
- "Fun is when we can joke around while we work and the teacher won't yell at us."

- "Fun is getting to laugh in class."

- "Fun is wondering what we're going to do and knowing it will be cool."

- "Fun is not being bored all the time."

- "Fun is when everyone is in a good mood and there's no stress."

- "Fun is when you forget what you're worried about."

- "Fun is when the teacher tries to make it interesting to learn."

- "Fun is when I know I understand and I get good grades."

- "Fun is when the teacher is excited about teaching and likes me."

- "Fun is not worrying that others in the class will tease you."

A classroom with an atmosphere of stress, fear of making mistakes, and pressure to please the teacher will shut down a child's ability to take risks, think creatively, and experience any delight and satisfaction from learning. This isn't a fun classroom, and it's not a happy environment in which to spend your day as a teacher, either.

When we put in place practices that hurt the child in order to ensure higher scores on tests, we are running counter to the wisdom or knowledge gathered today about how humans behave and function. When we structure weekly math tests for kindergarteners and weekly reading word count tests for second-graders and set aside crying rooms for those traumatized on big test days—all in the name of raising achievement—just who are we fooling? Aren't we saying that the only purpose of this "company" is to make a high return on the "investment," rather than to build the best "products"? And consider the fallout: low morale, the best teachers leaving the field, children who are crippled by low self-confidence and riddled with fear of failure or risk taking, and perhaps an artificial rise in scores at a terrible future price.

When you stop staring at your school's statistics and set your heart and mind to your vision and purpose for being in education, the statistics run behind trying to catch up with the passion. And when you do take a breath and turn around to look, you exclaim, "Oh my, how well those scores seem to be catching up with us!"

Fun Activities Versus Real Work

Many teachers fear that if their students were asked to do things that involved movement, playacting, props, or anything that veered off the norm, they would either flatly refuse to participate or act out and ruin the lesson. However, time and time again, students who are given the opportunity to be active participants prove these fears to be baseless.

Once that fear is overcome, next comes the question of how to transition from those engaging strategies to "real" work, the hard, serious work. The answer may be hard to swallow for some: students will do *any* work if it is planned well enough, set up for success, and broken down into understandable segments. Convincing teachers that active learning is a preferable mode of operation for sustained growth and achievement is at the heart of changing their mindsets about fun.

One point needs to be clear: activities that are fun only for the sake of being fun are deadly to educational growth. Using an engaging and fun lesson or strategy with no real learning goal, no follow-up, no connection to the scope and sequence of the curriculum to be covered is simply entertaining a class. That's dysfunctional fun, not effective teaching fun. Instead, use a highly engaging activity to set a strong positive memory in students' minds that can be quickly accessed and reinforced later. For example, to emphasize important parts of a book, ask groups of students to take one section each and turn it into dialogue with action notations where appropriate. Then have them present these scripts to the class by acting them out. The more visual and tactile and wrapped in a positive emotion the activity is, the better its staying power in children's memory banks (Jensen, 2003). With this long-term vision behind highly engaging activities, we avoid the pitfall of simply entertaining students instead of educating them.

Great Teachers Think Fun

While Cori Brewster and Jennifer Fager (2000) were visiting schools to compile information for their report *Increasing Student Engagement and Motivation: From Time-on-Task to Homework*, they observed third-grade teacher Lee McBride:

> Like many excellent teachers, Lee McBride doesn't do things in her classroom because someone told her to, or because some expert wrote about it. By her own admission, she teaches the way she does because it's the way she would want to learn. Learning is fun in her classroom. Not fun in a clichéd sense, but fun in a genuine kid kind of way. She knows that when kids enjoy learning, they are engaged in school. When preparing a lesson or unit for her third-grade class, she always asks herself questions like, "What do I want them to learn?" and "How do I want them to learn it?" She also considers what state and district standards require of her students, and with all this in mind, learning takes shape.

Lee McBride knows what all good teachers know: if the students aren't enjoying the learning, there isn't much learning going on. We could add that if the teacher isn't enjoying the teaching, there isn't much teaching going on, either.

Steps Toward Solutions

We need to change not how we act so much as how we think, that it is not about changing what we do so much as changing who we are. Fun is not an artificial action or set of beliefs that can be adopted. Fun must be woven into the fabric of the individual.

—Leslie Yerkes

Perhaps the best way to start examining our relationship with fun in our classrooms is to stop and reflect on how we feel about fun. Write out answers to the following prompts to see if you can unearth some of your thoughts and attitudes on this subject:

- What is the nature of fun? Does it exist in your classroom? When? Why? Why not?

- What did you think about the discussion of the relationship between work and fun?

- Has anyone ever tried to make you feel guilty about your students having too much fun in your room? Have you ever entertained negative thoughts about teachers whose students seem to be having fun in their classes?

- Make a list of ten times you have been aware of having fun with your class. Choose three to analyze: what happened to make it fun, what would be duplicable in the future, what ingredients were present, and just who was having fun—you, the whole class, some of them?

- Reread what students considered fun (pages 86–87). Choose a couple that really strike a chord with you. Write them on a sticky note, and attach it on your computer or plan book to remind you to incorporate these more often in your teaching.

- Ask your students what they think a fun class is like. Make a list of the best or most common replies, and use them as the subject of a class discussion. See how many could be implemented and what circumstances need to be in place for them to be effective. Keep an open mind, and have the class, not you, throw out inappropriate suggestions.

- Have certain rules, routines, or habits associated with the classroom become so solidified in your approach to teaching or ingrained in your students that they seem difficult and even senseless to consider changing? Pick one to change anyway.

Allow Fun Into Your Classroom

Let's say you do make the decision to have fun in your classroom. Here's what probably will happen: you will become more open and, yes, more vulnerable. Subtly you will begin to release control and see yourself as part of your class rather than separate from it. You will see yourself as working *with* them toward a goal rather than dictating to them from above. You will become less rigid with yourself and your students.

Keep in mind that you don't have to try to be funny. Being funny and having a fun classroom are not the same things at all. An atmosphere of fun in a classroom is created when you give yourself and your students permission to be your most authentic selves.

Add Novelty

Anything that breaks the routine of the expected is fun. Work at sprinkling as much novelty into your routine as you can. Later in the book, we will look more closely at the relationship between novelty and routine, but for now, here are some suggestions that might fit the bill:

- Make up special ceremonies to begin or end a unit and to honor students' outside accomplishments—in sports, Scouts, church activities, and so forth.

- Find real audiences for your students' projects, and invite them in or take the projects to them. Real audiences could be composed of younger students, senior citizens, the principal, or another class that you invite to come in and watch your students' presentations, for example.

- Surprise a student every day. For many students, simply talking to them about anything besides schoolwork is a welcome surprise. Remembering a birthday or commenting on a new haircut or piece of clothing will always surprise your students.

- Designate student card holders. Give the student a large red card to hold up if you are talking too long, a yellow card if the student is getting confused, and so forth.

- Bring in a soapbox that students are free to use if they feel something needs to be brought up to the class. Stand on it yourself to get something off your mind.

- Tap into your students' love of video games by having them try their hand at constructing one. Steer them to the Alliance for Young Artists & Writers contest (http://artandwriting.org), which opened up video games as a category for grades 7 through 12 in 2010.

- Consider challenging your students to follow the theory that fun is the best way to change behavior for the better. Go to www.thefuntheory .com/fun-theory-award to learn about the Fun Theory Contest. Show your students the remarkable examples of this fun theory in action by viewing the YouTube clips: the Piano Staircase, the World's Deepest Bin, and the Bottle Bank Arcade Machine are just a few samples of how fun changes behavior in public places. Have a contest of your own in the classroom for changing behaviors in your school with interesting, fun solutions.

- Instead of routinely answering the questions at the end of a chapter, tell the class that you think they would do as good a job as fancy text-book writers at constructing those questions. With guidelines (rubrics) that cover the areas you want covered, turn the usual assignment upside down, and have students write questions instead of answers. Tell them that the best ones will show up on tests later on in the unit. Students delight in the thought that they are challenging the system!

- Introduce the birthday bell. If a student tells you it is his or her birth-day, put the birthday bell on his or her desk. That student is then the special person of the hour, and when he or she wants to answer a question or get your attention, if the birthday bell is rung, go there first and make a big deal out of being totally at his or her service. Even high school students play right along with this and love ring-ing the bell to get you to go to their desks to see what they need. Actually, seldom will anyone create a nuisance by overdoing it. This is all in the name of fun, and they know it.

- Schedule a few ten-minute field trips. Field trips are usually so difficult to plan and process and organize these days that students don't really go on as many as they did years ago. There are many interesting opportunities on campus that merit a tiny field trip. After informing the office that you will be out of the room for the next ten to twenty minutes, have students fill out mock permission slips and sign them. Then lead them on your mini field trip around the building, on the grounds, or next to your grounds. For instance, you can take the stu-dents to see exhibits displayed by other classes in the halls.

- Breaking up the routine of the class period is priceless in many stu-dents' eyes. Go outside to take pictures in costumes that fit the set-tings of books you are reading. Use the cafeteria during off hours to do work on tables or prepare in groups for performances. Book the librarian to give your class a rundown of the newest books in the library. Before class officer elections or club recruiting days or elections for court kings and queens, the hallways are plastered with signs and notices. Sadly, many usually have a couple of grammatical and/ or spelling errors. Send students out in teams on a grammar police raid to see how many they can find. Give them only a short time, and warn them that any group that goes over the limit will be disqualified. The school, not simply your assigned room, is your classroom; use the entire facility. Using space creatively is fun!

- Get a wizard puppet, and play Ask the Wizard to review material. Have volunteers hold the wizard and answer the questions.

- Make up wacky awards, and dedicate a bulletin board to displaying them.

- Each school has an end-of-the-year awards ceremony, during which the same students seem to win most of the awards. Consider giving out your own awards for each class member before attending the assembly. This may be the only award some students get.

Reflection on Fun

Alfred Mercier said, "What we learn with pleasure, we never forget." Do you agree?

Write about your reactions to the topic of fun. What ideas could you have added to the solutions section of this chapter? List them. How will you use serious fun to engage and motivate your students?

_____

_____

_____

_____

_____

_____

_____

_____

_____

_____

_____

_____

_____

_____

One new strategy you might try out this week:

_____

Confidence

A person's level of confidence can often offset his or her native ability when it comes to performance. We have all known students who were able to do much better work but simply didn't see themselves as capable. On the flip side, we've also seen students with a more limited range of native talent who outperform other students because of their intense confidence in their own abilities. Increasing confidence levels in our charges is one of the most powerful gifts we can offer our students. In this chapter, we examine suggestions on how best to do this and how our own confidence levels play a part in those of our students.

First Thoughts on Confidence

This chapter deals with both student confidence and teacher confidence. What are some of your own thoughts and experiences with these topics?

_____

_____

_____

_____

_____

_____

_____

_____

_____

Notes From the Field

The following excerpt is from a personal journal entry written during a long-term coaching assignment at a high school.

Before school, a couple of teachers and I discussed how to help students who are not confident and are constantly receiving failing grades. These teachers feel their efforts at reaching some of these students are failing and that they, too, are experiencing real confidence issues. We talked about inserting activities that don't have students pitted against each other and instead are win-win opportunities for everyone.

During first period, I sat with Emmanual, a boy from Sudan, who was stuck trying to choose one of the three writing prompts his teacher had given the class. He just couldn't begin. I kept questioning him, teasing out ideas until he finally came up with a memory from when he was little. And did he ever come up with one! At the age of six, he accidentally burned down a neighbor's house, then ran away to a church and stayed there most of the night. When he went home, he said, his parents tried to get him to tell them what had happened, but he wouldn't admit the truth. . . . While telling the story, Emmanual became really animated and came up with great details.

I showed him how to do a web type of brainstorming. As he spoke, I motioned for him to write down a phrase or word on his paper that connected to one he had previously written. When his narrative was finished, we looked at the paper, and he was amazed. He said it shouldn't be hard at all to write the paper after this. He said he never thought he had anything to write about, but now he's confident he could do this again!

Before lunch while modeling a lesson using manipulatives, a tenth-grade student asked me if I ever taught kindergarten. I laughed, then I explained to the boy that those early year teachers have the right idea and I was indeed grabbing and adapting every good idea I saw from them. I told him that it is a proven fact that we learn and remember better if we engage all our senses. That is why I was giving his class pieces of sentences to move around on their desks, huge sentence clauses on butcher paper to hold up, and cheat sheets to use to better write their own sentences. He smiled at me and agreed with what I was doing.

Later that afternoon, the teacher came up to me and said that she loved how I answered that young man and that she wouldn't have been confident enough to have answered him so easily. She said she had read all the multi-intelligence material but really never made the transfer to the classroom, never even considered it until she saw what I was doing. This really amazed her. What I loved was that she *was really watching and reflecting on not only my behavior but hers as well. She said that the kind of remark that student made was one she always dreaded and probably the reason why she always second-guesses herself when considering the use of a strategy that is different from the norm. She saw me slay her dragon of dread—or if not slay him, at least put a dent in his scales!*

The Discussion

We've all experienced different kinds of confidence. There's huge, hunky, strong confidence that seems to fill us with so much anticipation—like a race-horse fidgeting in the starting gate—smothering any inkling of fear, begging us to act. Then there's the confidence draped more in hope than in assurance. This confidence knows it's reasonable to think all will turn out well. There's history behind this confidence that attests to a strong probability of success, yet it takes a consistent effort to fight off the little whispery voice that narrates what failure could be looming on the horizon. Finally, there's that confidence that has had little or no prior experience and needs to be propped up and supported by an outside figure who for some reason is sure you can accomplish something—someone who has not only hope but a groundswell of irresistible faith in your abilities. This is the confidence that we borrow from others until we have enough of our own. This is the confidence teachers lavish on their students—seeing what they are capable of long before they can see it, much less feel and experience it themselves. Confidence is one of the finest products of a well-run classroom.

In Sherman Alexie's (2009) wonderful young-adult novel *The Absolutely True Diary of a Part-Time Indian*, Junior's coach was just such a distributor. Junior had been told he would be guarding the best player on the opposing team and thought, "I had zero chance of competing directly with Rowdy. If I guarded him, he was going to score 70 points" (p. 188). Yet the coach kept saying, "You can do it":

> He didn't shout it. He whispered it. Like a prayer. And kept whispering again until the prayer turned into a song. And then, for some magical reason I believed him. . . . Do you understand how amazing it is to hear that from an adult? Do you know how amazing that is to hear from anybody? It's one of the simplest sentences in the world, just four words, but they're the four hugest words in the world when they're put together. You can do it. (p. 189)

Emmanual's Experience

The journal entry echoes this feeling of amazement a student experiences when an adult keeps saying, "You can do it." Emmanual usually succeeded in sitting alone despite the attempts of the teacher to see that everyone was posi-tioned in clusters of three or four. This class of around twenty-four students was filled with extroverted personalities that took all the teacher's energy and focus to keep on task. Emmanual never made any attempt to join in whole-class discussions, but he also never missed anything that was said. His lack of participation made his lack of confidence apparent.

The writing skills of many English learners are often painfully lacking. And the act of trying to put their thoughts into words—words that seem artificial to them—is itself a quite painful experience. Over the years, I have come to a simple yet important understanding about the relationship between build-ing confidence in these young writers and communicating a respect for their innate intelligence. Just because students cannot read well and cannot express themselves in our standard written language does not mean they are not intel-ligent thinkers. Sadly, we've all seen children's intelligences judged solely on their competency with English. Many educators agree that the major standard-ized tests are more a test of reading proficiency than of subject matter acquisi-tion. When we communicate that we really feel a student has a lot more going for him or her than can be measured at present by the testing mechanism, we will inevitably see the eyes light up, the bond form, and the resistance to get to work dissolve.

Emmanual, like many students, needed scaffolding tools to better see what his thoughts were and how his thoughts could be clustered together or even discarded if necessary. At this early stage in his writing, one tool was the web mapping technique; another tool was the coach who was stubbornly whisper-ing, "You can do it." The role of the coach or teacher is to prod the young ath-lete or scholar and move him or her from the "can't do" to the "can do" again and again.

Emmanual settled on the prompt of a childhood memory—the accidental fire. To get him started, I drew a little house in flames in the center of the paper. Then I simply kept asking him questions, and we added the answers in words or sketches on the paper. Why was he in the neighbor's house? Who were the neighbors? Where was everyone else? How did he get his hands on the matches? What was he thinking? What did he do when the flames started? What burned first? Where did he go? Could he see the house from there? What did he see? How long did he stay there? What part of the church did he hide in? Was he cold? Hungry? Crying? What was happening in the village? Were people looking for him? Who did he see? When did he decide to go back home? Why? What did he tell his family? Where did the family who had lost their house go? What was it like keeping that secret all these years? Looking back, how did he see the incident differently? We jotted down the answers he could provide. We talked about the dominant emotions that he had felt and whether that would be a good place to focus his narrative. I told him that the questions I asked were the kinds of questions he should ask himself when he brainstormed his next paper. This is how writers prepare, making it so much easier when they begin to write in earnest.

Emmanual didn't need me to sit next to him and pepper him with questions the next time he was given a writing assignment. He got the idea, and he had the knowledge and confidence necessary to believe that he could indeed succeed. He was ready to work on another skill now.

One of the primary jobs of educators is to recognize a student's unique set of abilities, strengths, and talents and not only point them out to the student but to support any effort that student might make in manifesting that talent. When teachers see that spark of desire, of possibility, they should rush to fan it into flame, to feed that spark with their own confidence. The more confidence students have, the better the quality of their performance.

Problems Stemming From a Lack of Confidence

Confidence is so basic to engagement that we often overlook it; we seldom think about it or put it on any checklist of things we need to pack. Yet confidence is a necessary part of any child's back-to-school equipment. A child facing school without any confidence is a runner without any running shoes, a cross-country biker without his bike. Confidence is necessary for the educational process to function properly. Yet many of our young come to us with a slight and tenuous degree of confidence, or it is quickly drained away as they enter our hallways.

Teachers are sometimes met with resistance when trying to build the confidence base of their students. An often-cited study conducted by Todd Risley and Betty Hart, who spent years researching the language of small children and their caretakers, reveals that at about age three, the typical child in a professional family hears thirty-two affirmative messages and five prohibitions per hour. This is a ratio of six encouragements to one discouragement. The typical child in a working-class family accumulates twelve affirmatives and seven prohibitions per hour, forming a ratio of about two encouragements to one discouragement. The average child in a family on welfare is subject to five affirmatives and eleven prohibitions per hour, constructing a ratio of about one encouraging message to every two discouraging ones (Risley & Hart, 1995).

This study provides a pretty clear picture of why some students may be so resistant to your confidence-building efforts. If a child is seldom encouraged at home and often hears negative statements, that child is skeptical when he or she hears a compliment or positive statement. That child thinks that you really don't know him or her very well; otherwise, you wouldn't be saying those encouraging things. It will take a great deal of consistent effort on your part for such a child to build enough trust in your judgment to begin to believe that what you say could possibly have some truth to it. In other words, you simply need to keep at it! Eric Jensen (2009) writes, "Hope changes brain chemistry, which influences the decisions we make and the actions we take. . . . Hopeful kids try harder, persist longer, and ultimately get better grades" (pp. 112–113). Building hope and confidence isn't a fuzzy extra; it's a fundamental necessity in closing any achievement gap and raising test scores across the board.

Kathie Marshall went back to an intervention classroom of sixth- and seventh-graders after serving as a literacy coach for six years. She was given a scripted reading curriculum and found herself "pushing students through a massive workbook each day." The students' general reaction was "It's booooooring!" Marshall tried to sidestep the scripted material with high-interest varied activities, because she felt that along with the goal of improving reading was "the equally important goal of providing my at-risk students with positive learning experiences. Many were already beaten down and convinced they were losers. Bringing some fun and win-win into the classroom equation would help them, however cautiously, to try once more" (Marshall, 2009).

Marshall asked her students—as she had done previously with all her at-risk students—just when they had lost interest in school. The students explained that they had first lost interest as early as second grade, when they were retained as the lowest performers. Many educators are finding that when students lose confidence in their ability to keep up, to perform as the system expects, they adopt one of two responses to school. Either they cave in and experience feelings of shame and guilt and lack self-value, ambition, self-discipline, and persistence, or they rebel and take on a hostile and uncooperative attitude to protect themselves from the system by not participating at all (Olson, 2009).

The Importance of Nonjudgmental Activities

Marshall stated that she felt a need to insert some "win-win into the classroom equation." This can be accomplished by including confidence-building activities—activities that don't have winners or losers, don't have grades assigned to them that rank students, but rather allow each student to feel competent and productive. Nonjudgmental activities are those that allow for a wide variance of product or performance without any judgment being imposed on its value. With so much assessing and ranking and judging in the school experience, it is easy to see how those who struggle with learning can get discouraged and burdened by feelings of inadequacy. Nonjudgmental activities serve to release the steam from the usual pressure-cooker environment of the classroom for many students.

Practice is the premier nonjudgmental activity, and it isn't occurring nearly enough in today's schools. Teachers are asked to evaluate, score, and record every single thing their students do in class. This request has become even more predominant since the electronic gradebook now can be instantly posted online, allowing parents to see and measure exactly how well their children are progressing. The idea of a more immediate check on progress than the traditional four times a year is definitely a good one, especially since immediate feedback is one of the most potent forms of student motivation. But a valid case needs to be made for the necessity of including a healthy supply of ungraded practice: activities that don't necessarily have to be intensely scrutinized or judged by the teachers.

Perhaps we can take a cue from the sports world. Coaches are always subjected to high-stakes evaluations. Every Saturday morning in the fall, football coaches' efforts and decisions are splashed across the hometown newspapers for everyone to read and critically review. Yet they know the value and place for practice. Students in classrooms also need time to hone their skills informally without worrying that their "grade" will ultimately be affected.

Instead of rushing too quickly with criticism or marks in a gradebook, we need to beef up our applause and celebration of the small, tenuous attempts that strengthen the confidence levels of our students. We need to consciously insert more opportunities for whole-class, nonjudgmental experiences where there are no winners and losers, no competition and ranking systems looming.

Teacher Confidence and Its Effects on the Classroom

One of the prevalent attitudes expressed by teachers as they see teaching coaches model strategies or lessons that call for a great deal of student participation and buy-in is that their students won't go for those strategies. But this is really a matter of teacher confidence. They are afraid they will be humiliated, that they will fail. This fear keeps them from taking risks. So it seems that before we attempt to build confidence in our students, we need to focus on building confidence in ourselves.

Change of any kind requires a safe environment and doesn't happen because some consultant comes sweeping in brandishing a handful of new ideas or strategies or takes a day to explain how to implement a new program the district has purchased. Teachers' confidence develops in an atmosphere of trust and safety, which is often generated by their peers. It works like this: the teacher who has the courage to try out a new strategy and finds it successful goes out into the hall, figuratively jumps up and down, tells the teachers next to her what just happened, and offers to give her neighbors copies of the lesson or strategy. *That* is what encourages the timid teachers to take a big step and try something new. Their trust in the fact that it is working for the person next door manufactures confidence. As the word spreads down the halls, the job of changing attitudes and combating fear gets easier and easier—strengthening teachers' faith in their own ability to step out of the entrenched routine and give growth a try.

However, peer input isn't always positive. A teacher's confidence can easily be wounded by fellow teachers who have adopted a predominately negative outlook—or by a couple of students voicing critical comments or by an administration that seems never to see one's efforts but never misses a slight transgression.

Despite many pundits' assertions that a teacher's effectiveness can be immediately measured and recorded through testing processes, the teaching experience does not always allow us to see the results of the day's efforts. Students are organic beings, and growth is not always able to be graphed and measured accurately. Much thinking needs to marinate inside the mind and can't be pulled out immediately for judgment. Unlike discrete skills, deeper learning and understanding isn't as easily assessed on a predetermined timetable. Because of this, teachers need a strong faith, a strong confidence, in their own abilities that can sustain them through those periods of gestation during which students' intellectual growth isn't always visible. Loss of confidence could keep a teacher from ever rising to his or her full potential. Self-doubt and second-guessing one's competencies often result in a strong aversion to taking any risks or trying new approaches.

A teacher is confident when he or she has been properly prepared to understand and deliver the content, is offered opportunities to further that preparation, and is not given an unreasonable schedule of classes or subjects to teach that strips the teacher of necessary time to adequately prepare. A teacher is confident when he or she has a wide assortment of strategies ready to deal with the diversity of needs that students exhibit. A teacher is confident when he or she is empowered to choose materials and pedagogy that will help students reach the standards and goals agreed upon by the state or province or district. An absence of any of the situations mentioned above handicaps the teacher and consequently the students as well.

A teacher who lacks the confidence to try new strategies for fear of making a mistake will most likely pass this fear on to his or her students. Low confidence will eat up a teacher's ability to hold high expectations for his or her students. Since a teacher's level of confidence will impact that of his or her students, working on improving both in tandem is the best route to take.

Steps Toward Solutions

Phil Schlecty might say that student engagement depends on providing students with meaningful work. Ron Ferguson might answer that student engagement is contingent on the relationship the teacher establishes with the students. Robert Marzano might suggest that student engagement is contingent on the quality of instruction in the classroom. In addition to all three of these, there is also the factor of whether the teacher believes in the students' abilities to accomplish challenging work. I embrace the phrase that engaging work is rigorous or challenging to the student, establishes relevance to the life or interests of the student, and is embraced because of the relationship with the teacher who establishes the tasks. Teachers who engage students at this level also have a fundamental belief in the abilities of their students to achieve at high levels. Effective teachers manage these criteria and more in order to ensure their students are learning and performing at higher levels every day.

—Stephanie Hirsh

Student confidence is a major key to increasing student engagement. Look at the ways you already go about boosting your students' confidence. Once you have a clearer understanding of how you are currently making positive strides, you can easily build on your own good practices.

Take a Closer Look at Confidence Builders

Make a list of how you boost student confidence in your daily contacts. Then look at the following list, and select a few to try out:

- Make opportunities for small successes; avoid failure experiences.
- Set up nonjudgmental activities that surprise students with their innate competency, and build on these.

- Praise successes both individually and in front of the class.

- Foster a relationship that says, "I believe in you. I have faith in you. I'll help you. I'm here for you."

- Cultivate a tolerance for mistakes. Perhaps allow your students to sometimes mark their first and second choices in multiple-choice quizzes, and give half credit if the second one is correct. Make sure this tolerance is obvious in your voice and attitude.

- Emphasize process rather than product and provide grades for both. Keep folders of your students' work and refer to them to show the students how they have progressed and what they've learned. Some schools keep folders and send them on to the next grade level so that students can compare how they are doing at any time with how they were doing in the beginning of the year.

- Purposefully include a wide variety of activities in your lessons to discover strengths, intelligences, and interests, and play to those strengths.

- Tell stories of hope about people your students can relate with.

- Do not set limits on learning. (A mother doesn't tell her child, "You only have one year to learn how to walk because that's what the pacing guide says; that's the norm.")

- Avoid comparisons and competitions among kids in which some are labeled losers and others winners.

- Ask students to share their hopes and goals in class.

- Avoid a fixation on standardized test scores. Such a fixation can result in low scorers experiencing intense guilt and self-hatred for letting the school down.

- Validate and honor abilities and efforts. This gives students the courage to take risks in other things.

- Find out what your students are good at outside of school, and use that knowledge to relate and connect to new information and to offer suggestions for projects and writing prompts that center on their interests.

- Ask students to teach you something they know but you don't.

- Tell students specifically why they are capable of succeeding.

Build Confidence Through Writing

A relatively simple activity that has been documented to work to build confidence and raise the proficiency of low-achieving middle school students is a writing prompt that asks students to choose a few values they feel they have from a list of qualities and skills such as sense of humor, athletic ability, singing talent, creativity, and so forth. The students are then asked to explain why these values are important. They write on the same prompt three or four times during the school year. Benedict Carey (2009) of the *New York Times* reports,

> Researchers had found that such exercises reduced stress and the fear of failure in some students. By the end of eighth grade, among black students who were struggling, those who had expressed in writing their most important values had an average G.P.A. that was 0.4 points higher than those who had not. . . . The assignment reminded students that their entire self-worth was not riding on a single test result.

Set up this assignment for your own students. Perhaps begin with a short brainstorming activity with the whole class on what traits, qualities, values, and skills they might possess. Write the suggestions on the board as students offer them. The more they can offer, the easier it will be for everyone to pick a few that pertain to them and to then write.

Teach Students About Their Brains

Students love to learn and talk about themselves. They are often very attentive when being shown how their brains operate, why they act or react the way they do, and all the other brain research we are privy to these days. It's like they are being shown the secret manual to how they work! Set aside time to discuss the brain and address the issues of self-confidence, self-esteem, and positive thinking.

Also discuss the body and how "stress and repetitive negative internal talk leads to the release of the hormones cortisol and adrenaline, which reduce short-term memory and bring about tunnel vision and focus necessary for safety—but counter-productive for education" (Burns & Sinfield, 2004, p. 49). Students will find it easier to deal with these issues if they discover that others are carrying around the same fears and feelings of inadequacy that they are.

You are the cheerleader for those in your class who are unsure, are insecure, and feel like failures. Research proves that your expressions of confidence can increase a child's self-confidence. Your job is to supply that confidence until your students are strong enough to fall back on their own. Train yourself to see them as they could possibly be in the future rather than how they currently are and reflect for them a vision of a capable and gifted person.

Avoid Failure

Since failure leads to self-hatred, shame, and a lack of desire to take any risk or put out any effort, construct situations in the classroom that avoid failure to ensure student engagement and ultimately student achievement. What is confidence but faith, a rebirth of hope in one's possibilities, and the seed of a nurturing self-love—three qualities that are extremely valuable and worth demonstrating!

Assign the Five-Minute Poster

The five-minute poster is an example of a nonjudgmental activity that I picked up from a young teacher to address the resistance students show to taking risks and trying new things, all from the fear of possibly getting it wrong. This enjoyable activity clusters skill building with attitude adjusting. Each student has a piece of colored paper, a cut-out mistake from the book *Mistakes That Worked: 40 Familiar Inventions and How They Came to Be* by Charlotte Flotz, and access to markers. Tell them they have five minutes to complete their posters. Here are the directions: (1) read the article, (2) label the paper on top with the mistake, (3) draw a simple sketch of the item, and (4) write three to four bulleted, interesting facts about the mistake. If they get finished before the five minutes are up, then they can make an appealing border around the edges of the paper.

Give out shorter mistakes to slower readers to level the playing field. It really shouldn't take much longer than five minutes to complete the exercise. However, if you see that the students need another minute, just wait a little longer to call "time's up." In groups of four to five, each student explains orally what happened in the reading and uses the poster as a graphic to highlight the presentation. Afterwards, ask for volunteers from each group to present to the whole class.

With this exercise, students are summarizing, illustrating, and choosing facts they want to share. They can see that it doesn't take a full class period to get a job done; it only takes a short time, in fact. This exercise could be used with any subject matter that has enough pieces of information that each student has a different piece to share with the group. Collect books with short passages, sets of information cards, and books with biographies. This makes a great frontloading activity for any new unit of study, immersing the class in a variety of facts, people, and ideas—and quickly.

Build Confidence in Your Colleagues

Do you help build the confidence of your fellow teachers? Make a list of the ways in which you can invest in the hope and confidence of your school's faculty and staff members. By building another teacher's confidence, you are affecting every student on that teacher's roster!

Make a concerted effort to share new and effective strategies you develop or come across with your colleagues, and resolve to provide a listening ear to those who need one. Build the confidence of less-experienced teachers by offering to work with them on developing lessons and activities and following up by comparing notes on how things are working out. It's easy to get so wrapped up in our own classes that we have little time or interest in helping out our fellow teachers. This doesn't take much time, but it does take a generous spirit.

Reflection on Confidence

Recall your "first thoughts." Did you think about student confidence or teacher confidence or both? Which do you feel is the easiest to address? Which is the hardest to change? How will you use confidence to engage and motivate your students?

_____

_____

_____

_____

_____

_____

_____

_____

_____

_____

_____

_____

_____

_____

_____

One new strategy you might try out this week:

_____

Attitudes

Most students' attitudes toward school are a result of their perceptions of their abilities to master material, their likes or dislikes of subjects or instructional methods, and their positive or negative views toward the educational experience as a whole. This chapter discusses the need and ability to change some of the attitudes about learning that might hold a student back from doing his or her best work or becoming engaged. Changing an attitude is like moving a fulcrum on a diving board; just a little shift creates a big difference.

First Thoughts on Attitudes

Our attitudes toward ourselves regarding our strengths and weaknesses often determine how eager or reluctant we are to try new things, invest in risk taking, and exert effort. Take a few minutes to think about how your attitude toward your ability to succeed in school has played a role in your behaviors, your choices, and your performance. Try to think of a situation in which your attitude blocked you from making a specific choice.

_____

_____

_____

_____

_____

_____

_____

Notes From the Field

In 1991, Arthur Costa published a list of twelve "habits of mind" (discussed in detail later in the chapter), or indicators of intelligent behavior. This list was used to prompt students to reflect on their intelligence. The following is a student's explanation of five habits that she exhibits in her life.

> Of the twelve intellectual indicators, five are my strengths. My strongest indicator is referred to as "questioning and problem posing." If I want to know something, I ask. When somebody tells me something that doesn't make sense to me, I have them explain it in terms that I can understand. "What if" questions are frequently popping up in my conversations.
>
> After that, wonderment, inquisitiveness, curiosity, and the enjoyment of problem solving is my next strongest indicator. I enjoy sitting down and trying to determine the answer to problems. I love to sit down with math homework and solve the different equations for the day.
>
> In addition, I can draw on past knowledge and apply it to new situations. For instance, if I know that my response to someone else started problems between us, the next time I will respond differently. I compare situations and apply the knowledge of the consequences of old decisions to make a wiser choice.
>
> Next, I show persistence. When I start something, I finish it no matter how long it takes. I use as many methods or sources that are available to accomplish my tasks. I sometimes have to leave my project alone for a while, but I always go back and finish it.
>
> Last of all, I can listen to others with understanding and empathy. I understand that everyone is different and am able to use that in listening to others to detect feelings and emotional states. I can reword what one person is saying to explain it to someone else.

The Discussion

The emphasis on grades and test scores as signs of intelligence has been responsible for many children assuming the false attitudes that they are lacking in native ability, that they are deficient as human beings, and that those competencies that they do possess really don't count or amount to much in the eyes of society. Students who believe that they aren't smart and never will be are often difficult to engage in challenging, rigorous class work. Many of the efforts that succeed in motivating classes to participate wholeheartedly in lessons don't work with these students. A student's level of engagement is dependent upon his or her self-concept, and no number of bells and whistles, external rewards, or surface quick fixes can change a child's attitude toward himself or herself. The fix must go deeper. A powerful attitude-changing activity with students is a discussion on the topic of what intelligence really is and how we can tell if a person is intelligent without looking at his or her test scores, IQ, or report card grades.

Habits of Mind

Costa's habits of mind resulted from a study of the attributes of intelligent, successful problem solvers in many walks of life, which Costa and Bena Kallick compiled for the book *Developing Minds*, now in its third edition. In an interview for the *Journal of Advanced Academics*, Costa explained, "These are the habits that cause people to be successful in life, in careers, in marriage and family, as well as in academic pursuits such as college" (Richards, 2007).

The list used in the previously mentioned activity came out years before much work had been published on the brain and its functions and contained only twelve habits. The number of habits started at seven in 1984 and grew to sixteen by 2007. Following is Costa and Kallick's (2009) current list of sixteen habits of mind that designate intelligent behavior:

1. Persisting
2. Thinking and communicating with clarity and precision
3. Managing impulsivity
4. Gathering data through all senses
5. Listening with understanding and empathy
6. Creating, imagining, and innovating
7. Thinking flexibly
8. Responding with wonderment and awe
9. Thinking about thinking (metacognition)
10. Taking responsible risks
11. Striving for accuracy
12. Finding humor
13. Questioning and posing problems
14. Thinking interdependently
15. Applying past knowledge to new situations
16. Remaining open to continuous learning

Students are always fascinated with any information that sheds light on how they think, why they act the way they do, and how to better themselves. They will be surprised and fascinated to learn that these habits of mind reveal a person's intelligence. You will likely hear questions such as: "Where is the item that says, 'Takes tests well and scores high'?" "Where is the item that says, 'Gets all As on report cards'?" After the initial surprise that the list doesn't include those elements, the class focus turns to what is actually on this list and how many of these qualities students can truthfully say they possess. Then you'll hear responses such as: "Everyone tells me I'm a good listener." "My mom says I'm pretty stubborn because I always stick to something I start; I never give up. Does that mean I have persistence?" "I can't believe that humor is a sign of intelligence! I see humor in most situations." "I can't stand making mistakes in my homework. Does that mean I am striving for accuracy?" "What does 'managing impulsivity' mean?" And the questions and responses keep coming and coming.

When students see that they possess traits and attributes that are considered intelligent—skills that are appreciated within our society—they have a broader view of their personal intelligence and a broader sense of self-worth, resulting in increased student confidence and achievement. To reinforce the importance of these qualities of intelligent behavior, post the list up on the wall alongside the list of standards and the school code of behavior.

The list can also be applied to teachers. More important than a grade point average, a master's degree, or years of experience in the effectiveness of a teacher to raise student scores are the traits of perseverance, flexibility, reevaluating past performance, questioning, taking responsible risks, listening, managing impulsivity by staying focused, responding to life with wonderment and awe, and striving for accuracy. A decade of data on quality teacher performance accumulated by Teach for America has revealed many of the same traits. These qualities are used by Teach for America to determine which recruits will have the best chance for success and so should be hired (Ripley, 2010). Once we recognize those traits that allow us to function better and produce better results in our classrooms, we are likely to use them more consistently.

Changing the Belief That Intelligence Is Static

A powerful change in attitude capable of increasing a person's level of effort, motivation, and consequent achievement is the change from believing that a person's intelligence is fixed to understanding that a person's intelligence can grow and increase. If a child believes that he or she just isn't smart and never will be, there's very little reason to exert effort.

Carol Dweck, a leading researcher in the field of motivation, studied these fixed and growth mindsets in seventh-grade students for a two-year period and stated, "We saw among those with the growth mindset steadily increasing math grades over the two years. But that wasn't the case for those with the so-called fixed mindset. They showed a decrease in their math grades" (Trudeau, 2007).

Dweck (2008) then wondered if it were possible to change this fixed mindset by educating children about how brains grow when a person thinks something new. In her next study, children were taught how the brain grows branches of connections, called dendrites, making the point that the children were capable of getting smarter, that being smart was definitely within their control.

After this mini neuroscience course on the workings of the brain, Dweck said, when students studied, they visualized little dendrites growing in their heads. Soon they changed their attitudes toward the brain. No longer did they see it as a fixed, static blob; it was now an ever-growing muscle that became stronger and stronger when exercised. This knowledge changed their motivation. Dweck found that "the students were energized by the idea that they could have an impact on their mind." She went on to speak about a young boy who was the "ringleader of the troublemakers" who, "with tears in his eyes, said, 'You mean, I don't have to be dumb?'" (Dweck, 2008, p. 219).

Another important insight that came from these studies is how to deal with high-achieving students who have lost their motivation. If children are praised too often for being smart, they will want to keep that status and will often balk at taking risks for fear of making a mistake and looking foolish (Dweck, 2008). Many teachers of high-track/honors students or gifted students are well aware of this side of the motivation coin.

One way to praise an intelligent child is to praise that child's *efforts*, not his or her *intelligence*. A teacher had a banner over her blackboard that read: "If you are not out of your comfort zone, you aren't learning anything!" During particularly challenging work, she would ask the class, "Are you out of your comfort zone yet?" And when they groaned, "Yes," she would applaud their efforts and tell them how well they were doing. Breaking down the attitude that learning has to be comfortable and that any uncomfortable experience is to be avoided allows students to extend their efforts longer and sustain their levels of perseverance dramatically.

Learning Processes Affect Attitude

Attitudes about one's ability to learn and succeed can be strongly influenced by whether an artificial, narrow approach or a broader, more natural approach to learning is applied. Researchers Geoffrey Caine and Renate Caine (2009), directors of the Natural Learning Research Institute, state that when the natural learning approach is neglected, students form false attitudes—mostly negative—about themselves as competent, capable learners. These attitudes are later reflected in poor self-esteem and low motivation. Caine and Caine report:

> Most education in the United States settles for a very limited conception of learning, usually framed in terms of memorization, and the development of basic skills such as reading. Even though standards often call for the development of understanding, in practice teaching is for memorization. . . . The essential problem is that much of the learning that occurs naturally has been excluded from schools, so that learning from life and learning in schools have, to a very large extent, been divorced. When natural learning is embraced, many unused capacities of all children can be accessed and developed.

Caine and Caine's learning principles can be viewed in a wheel formation on their website (www.cainelearning.com/files/Wheel.html). The twelve basic principles of learning are:

1. All learning engages the physiology.
2. The brain/mind is social.
3. The search for meaning is innate.
4. The search for meaning occurs through patterning.
5. Emotions are critical to patterning.
6. The brain/mind processes parts and wholes simultaneously.
7. Learning involves both focused attention and peripheral perception.
8. Learning always involves conscious and unconscious processes.
9. We have at least two ways of organizing memory: an autobiographical memory system and a set of systems for rote memory.
10. Learning is developmental.
11. Complex learning is enhanced by challenge and inhibited by threat associated with helplessness.
12. Each brain is uniquely organized. (Caine Learning Center, 2010)

You have likely tried to guide students' minds to more than just a memorized grasp of information. Many of us use most of our creative energy not in making bulletin boards but in making authentic connections between complex concepts and what our children already know and experience in their

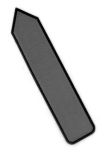

everyday worlds. In this hunt for better connections, we discover organic methods of learning that we all use but don't often relate to the formal classroom experience. We use our battery of soft skills—helping students feel less stressed, building relationships with them that foster trust and cooperation, providing room for social experiences among classmates, putting forth the effort to match assignments to the unique personalities and ability levels of those in our charge, and inserting as much meaning into our lessons as possible. Whenever a teacher applies natural learning methods to the classroom, that teacher not only engages the students' curiosity, but also guarantees a deeper understanding of the material.

Another effort at classifying educational behavior that serves to impact students' attitudes about themselves as learners is Benjamin Bloom's classification of levels of intellectual behavior important in learning—commonly referred to as Bloom's taxonomy. Educators agree that students need to master higher-order thinking skills and use these skills as often as possible if they are to grow to be thoughtful, competent adults. Bloom's taxonomy of higher-order thinking skills (HOTS) is standard material in most teacher education classes and consequently on Praxis tests—a qualifying hurdle for teacher certification.

The original levels of Bloom's taxonomy, beginning with the lowest, were: knowledge, comprehension, application, analysis, synthesis, and evaluation. These were revised by Lorin Anderson, a former student of Bloom, in the 1990s. The new terms are defined as:

- Remembering: retrieving, recognizing, and recalling relevant knowledge from long-term memory.
- Understanding: constructing meaning from oral, written, and graphic messages through interpreting, exemplifying, classifying, summarizing, inferring, comparing, and explaining.
- Applying: carrying out or using a procedure through executing, or implementing.
- Analyzing: breaking material into constituent parts, determining how the parts relate to one another and to an overall structure or purpose through differentiating, organizing, and attributing.
- Evaluating: making judgments based on criteria and standards through checking and critiquing.
- Creating: putting elements together to form a coherent or functional whole; reorganizing elements into a new pattern or structure through generating, planning, or producing. (Anderson & Krathwohl, 2001, pp. 67–68)

Teaching students about these thinking skills falls in line with teaching them about their brains. The more they know about how they function as human beings, the easier it is to convince them to take risks, put out more sustaining effort, and face challenges without succumbing to fight-or-flight behavior throughout the year. If we can show them just how natural it is for them to use these higher-order thinking skills, they will find that the higher the level, the more interesting it is to use. This understanding makes a tremendous difference in students' attitudes toward answering and discussing higher-order questions during a class. Instead of dreading this activity, students often anticipate it with a feeling of competence.

An effective method of helping students experience thinking at all of Bloom's levels and see how capable they are of participating in higher-level thinking is to use material that is engaging to all students at any level of academic skill. This serves to level the playing field for the discussion. Since studies have found that from 65 percent up to 80 percent of today's learners could be considered visual learners (Bradford, 2004), using a visual as the content for your lesson on Bloom's taxonomy usually works well. A sample lesson bringing the taxonomy to life for students is included in the Steps Toward Solutions portion of this chapter.

Both Caine and Caine's natural learning principles and Bloom's classification of thinking skills can increase our understanding of how we function intellectually. Since an attitude is a cognitive thought formed through experience and influences our behavior, giving students the experience of working with this knowledge about themselves should result in behaviors that are positive and will lead to a fuller level of engagement in their studies.

Teachers' Attitudes

Although this chapter deals primarily with how students better engage in the learning process if they come to it with a more positive attitude—an attitude that gives a student hope that he or she has a chance at succeeding—we mustn't overlook the importance of teachers' attitudes. If a teacher doesn't believe that students' brains can grow, if a teacher has mentally labeled certain students as "dumb" or "incorrigible," all the activities in the world won't convince those students otherwise. Students pick up on the beliefs and attitudes of their teachers much faster than they do on the degree of difficulty or the focus of an activity.

A high school math teacher made a new seating chart every couple of weeks according to how her students scored on the latest test. The front of the room was populated with the highest scoring students and the back of the room with the lowest scoring or failing students. Her attention and positive body language was always aimed at those first couple of rows while her disdain for those back-row occupants was immediately and shockingly visible. When asked about her seating arrangement, she responded that she had no time for or interest in those who couldn't do the work, and she felt her system just might shame some of them into working harder and producing better test results. This wasn't the case. Students tried to under-score each other to get the last seats.

If emotions are contagious, so are attitudes. A more productive approach for that teacher might have been convincing students that they are capable of getting smarter, that their actions and effort can make a distinct difference in their learning, to provide a boost to their motivation and ultimately their achievement. This is an important lesson for any teacher who wants to engage his or her students.

Contagious Attitudes: From Teacher to Students

Just as children pick up the same fears as their parents—a mother screams when she sees a spider, and her daughter does the same—so too do young students pick up the fears and attitudes of their teachers.

Remember the Barbie doll that said, "Math is tough!"? A public outcry spearheaded by the American Association of University Women quieted down the Mattel doll in a matter of three months. The *attitude* that girls have a harder time with math than boys, though, hasn't been quieted down that easily. A study published in the *Proceedings of the National Academy of Sciences* suggests that teachers themselves are perpetuating this stereotype. If a female teacher—and 90 percent of elementary teachers in the United States are female (Beilock, Gunderson, Ramirez, & Levine, 2010)—has a sense of anxiety about math, by the end of a year in her classroom, girls who did not enter her room with the belief that math is easier for boys than for girls will not only have picked it up, but will also be scoring significantly lower than those girls who were not exposed to teachers with this attitude. This study is significant in that it is the first both to examine the math attitudes of teachers and to show that those feelings can spread to students with the result of undermining their ability to perform (Beilock et al., 2010).

Not only are emotions contagious in a classroom as discussed in chapter 2, but the subtle feelings teachers hold concerning the subject matter and the students' ability to master that subject matter are just as contagious.

Our Attitudes Toward Our Bodies

Our own experiences of schooling have a tremendous influence on how we picture the normal classroom experience. They color our judgment of what is proper, what should be the norm, and what is unacceptable, and they shape our attitudes unless actively challenged and questioned. Many of us picture classrooms with rows of desks and a teacher at the front of the room, quiet work on sheets of problems or questions at the end of textbooks' chapters, occasional recitation or going to the blackboard to work a problem or correct a faulty sentence, and copious notes copied from overhead projector magnifications.

Many of these experiences run counter to what is considered to be healthy learning patterns today. The body has been seen as an unnecessary appendage to the serious work of educating the brain. The body has been seen as needing sustained control and discipline so that the brain can be accessed. The body—especially that of a squirming little boy—has been seen as an object in need of medicating so that we can more easily focus on our jobs as educators in peace and quiet. Now we know that both the body and mind are responsible for learning and can't be separated. We are aware of the physiological effects of stress, test anxiety, environment, poverty, nutrition, movement, natural growth phases, and such that can inhibit or aid the mind's ability to learn. We are urged by science and good common sense to take the whole child into account when setting up the optimal conditions for education. Our attitudes toward the classroom experience and the role our bodies play in the learning process need to be reconsidered in light of what we know today about our hierarchy of needs and how movement can facilitate learning (Maslow, 1954; Jensen, 2000; Lengel & Kuczala, 2010).

Applying what we are discovering about the important connection between the body and learning to our daily classroom actions is not easy. It's never easy to buck any internalized default template of attitudes that have been developed over years of exposure. So here is a simple place to begin: add a kinesthetic dimension to your normal routines. Having students engage in movement is a practical way to develop class cohesion. This is true for all age levels and not just the younger students in our charge. Authors Traci Lengel and Mike Kuczala (2010) write that movement offers the following benefits:

- Providing the brain with a much needed break
- Improving communication and listening skills
- Providing an opportunity for problem solving and higher-order thinking
- Offering an environment that promotes laughter and fun while engaging learners

- Improving motivation and discipline
- Heightening students' interest in attending and participating in class
- Building relationships and a general concern for one another
- Developing a sense of belonging
- Improving self-esteem (p. 7)

Building in opportunities for students to move during the school day results in better physical and mental health and doesn't cost a penny for the district or the individual teacher. The rewards from implementing such opportunities are also apparent in better achievement and the formation of constructive attitudes in children that should last a lifetime.

Steps Toward Solutions

If you don't like something change it; if you can't change it, change the way you think about it.

—Mary Engelbreit

We've talked in detail about the importance of the teacher's relationship to the class as a whole and to students as individuals. A great deal of those relationships is based on the fundamental attitudes a teacher brings with him or her into the classroom. Use the following list to examine your personal attitudes covering a variety of areas associated with your teaching:

- Take time to reflect on what you really think about the current research on effective methods to improve student learning, about the reason for the emphasis on learning styles, and about the need for active participation and meaningful tasks. Do you buy in to these ideas, or do you tell yourself that they are inferior to the direct teaching style you use?

- Pay attention to how you feel toward students on your roster who come from a different culture than yours. Do you hold any biases against students you currently teach?

- Examine whether you feel children from poverty are by nature not smart or not interested in learning. Do you give up on them and blame their failure on outside factors such as parent disinterest, lack of skills, or environmental causes?

- Think about your attitude toward gender and learning. Does your body language and patterns of calling on children to answer say anything about your basic attitude toward girls' and boys' learning abilities?

- Listen to your discussions in the lunchroom, and see if you are in the habit of calling academically proficient students the "good kids" and the low-performing students the "bad kids." Do you mix the language of morality with academic ability? Do you give students with better grades more leeway than those with low grades?

Change Attitudes About Intelligence

The following exercises serve to change students' attitudes about their abilities to think and respond intelligently. The first exercise results in a broadened understanding of what intelligence is and how it is demonstrated in everyday life:

1. Have students work in small groups and go down the list of Costa and Kallick's sixteen habits of mind, defining what each of the attributes actually is and how each could be visible in everyday life.

2. Then ask the students to individually circle five that they have exhibited at some time or another.

3. Next, ask the students to write about these five and give reasons and/or examples of how they know they have these traits, such as the essay that appears in the Notes From the Field section.

This exercise is beneficial in several ways. It demonstrates reflective thinking and leads the writers to alter their attitudes about their own worth and potential. It gives students a new perspective and provides a new basis for their judgments of one another. It shows the students that you have a strong respect for abilities that aren't indicated by test scores. What the students reveal in these short essays can also supply you with a depth of knowledge that can be used throughout the year to offer encouragement and support that immediately rings true and is considered legitimate praise by the most skeptical child.

Many students believe they are not smart enough to succeed and decide not to put forth the effort, setting themselves up for sure failure. Often the problem holding them back isn't their intelligence but their inability to express themselves in written form. The following activity uses a nonlinguistic subject matter and attempts to level the playing field for those handicapped by language constraints. Bloom's taxonomy is the foundation for the exercise.

Everyone needs to be able to see the picture (fig. 7.1). Make sure the projector light is bright enough and the class setup makes it easy for everyone to see the screen. Here are the directions:

1. Ask the students to pair with a partner.

2. Direct the students to mentally cut the picture into four sections— mentally draw lines down and across the middle.

Figure 7.1: Reading a picture with higher-order thinking.
Source: Illustration by Leon Zernitsky. Used with permission.

3. Ask the students to make a list of what they see in the top right section, sharing with their partners. Then they share as a group and add anything not already mentioned to their lists.

4. Do this for each quadrant, and then do it for the picture as a whole. Provide ideas on what the symbols might stand for. For example, the graphs could represent math; the road could be the information

highway; and the computers could represent technology. Students come up with many other ideas. You and your class have just read the picture. Now you're ready to begin the HOTS in earnest.

5. Explain that the first level of Bloom's taxonomy is the fact or knowledge level. Ask the students to write down five items in the picture and then share their choices with their partners.

6. The second level is comprehension. Ask the students to give the picture a title and share with their partners. This is a good way to see if students comprehend the picture.

7. For the third level, application, ask the students to explain to their partners how this painting could possibly apply to them and their lives, giving as many examples as possible.

8. For the fourth level, analysis, ask the students to analyze their titles and give a reason why their titles are perfect. Ask them to be specific.

9. Next, for level five, synthesis, discuss suggestions for changes that the artist could make in the painting to make it more appropriate as a mural for your school's entrance. Listen to as many ideas from the entire group as time allows.

10. Finally, for the sixth level, evaluation, ask the students to tell their partners how they would evaluate the ability of the artist to communicate what they have decided is his main idea in the picture. Ask the students to determine some of the picture's weaknesses and strengths.

Following this activity, discuss each level of higher-order thinking, including the suggestions, reasons, and details that students gave while exploring each level.

After you have thoroughly gone through the exercise, praise the students for working their way through all the levels of higher-order thinking. Point out that they have just proven that all the levels are within their grasp.

Pass out Bloom's Taxonomy Verbs (page 128), and talk about the types of questions that are associated with each level. Most students will say that the first-level questions are always hardest since they can't remember all the facts or get them mixed up. Students often feel that the higher-level verbs—such as *compare, debate, predict, propose, design, demonstrate, rate, estimate, compose,* and so forth—and their associated questions are the most interesting to answer and work with.

Show students that *higher order* does not always mean "more difficult." Here is an example of a high-level question that is easy: "Which movie did you like more, *WALL-E* or *Cars*? Why?" And here is an example of a low-level directive that is hard: "Write an essay explaining the decline and fall of the Roman Empire, incorporating at least five of the seven causes discussed in class from the writings of Gibbon and Toynbee." The basic difference in high- and low-order thinking is what happens in the mind. With low-order thinking, we are remembering and regurgitating. With higher-order thinking, we are determining what we can do, say, and make from the information. Higher levels are far more alive and engaging for the mind!

For the next activity, the students are to make up their own test and answers for a rather significant piece of material the class has been studying. This will serve as the major test on this material.

Here are the directions for composing the test: students are to create five level-one questions in any format—true or false, fill in the blank, matching—and then create one question from the list of verbs for each of the other levels. The point value of each level matches its difficulty—remembering = 1 point; understanding = 2 points; applying = 3 points; and so on. (Of course, when these tests are scored, the final value of each question will be much higher than these numbers.)

Students will ask questions you would never think they would ask. The variety and depth of the thinking that children exhibit when the framework allows for such thinking are amazing. Explain to them that our brains are built to work and enjoy the challenge of higher-order thinking. Our brains weren't constructed to just accumulate facts but rather to put facts together, to make and pick out patterns, and to solve problems and create solutions we haven't even considered yet. That's why we enjoy the higher levels so much more than the lower ones. Sadly, it seems that the majority of the questions teachers ask students are in the lowest level, which means they never really stimulate the brain in an engaging manner. It is estimated that 90 percent of all test questions asked in the United States are in a low level—knowledge and comprehension (Wilen, 1992).

The two activities in this section—orally going through the thinking levels using a picture rather than a written text as the content, and using the levels to formulate an important test—give the students a feeling that they have the capacity and ability to mentally handle the HOTS. They are now ready to try out their higher-order thinking skills on more challenging material with far more confidence than before. When students believe that they are indeed capable of handling higher-order thinking skills, their attitude toward their ability to succeed in school is much more positive.

Build Brains With Play-Doh

As is often the case in getting an important point across to children, just telling them that their brains are alive and growing, capable of getting smarter
and smarter, isn't enough. A far better method is to use a couple of highly visible, hands-on demonstrations that help children cement this idea into their
thinking. The exercises following were part of the material we used during the
Missouri Literacy Academy Project (2003–2008):

1. **The Fact**: Brains that aren't challenged to think don't grow many
    dendrites.

    The Visual: Bring in a small tree branch with only a few shoots
    and no leaves. Also bring in a bunch of broccoli. Pass around both
    objects, and explain how constantly thinking and making connec-
    tions between new material and ideas you already have will pro-
    duce broccoli rather than dead, barren sticks. (After a teacher used
    this activity, his students referred to "making broccoli" whenever a
    lesson or activity was challenging and pushed them to think harder
    than usual. The saying caught on and became part of their class-
    room culture of communication.)

    The Point: You can and do have control over your brain's growth.

2. **The Fact**: Stress, fear, or overexcitement will close down the brain's
    ability to remember or think effectively. If our emotions aren't in bal-
    ance, new information gets dumped from the limbic system before
    it ever reaches the neocortex and the cortex, which is where we do
    our thinking.

    The Visual: To show just how incoming information doesn't have a
    chance of ever reaching the brain if emotions are not balanced, hold
    a two-liter soda bottle with holes all over it over a waste basket or
    bucket, pour water into it, and explain to the students that the water
    is what the teacher is trying to teach and the bottle is the limbic
    system in their brains, and it is spilling all the content out because
    it's too angry, scared, happy, or despondent—too much of any emo-
    tional state. Then fill the bottle with little pieces, such as candy or
    pebbles, that represent the information that stays in the brain when
    our emotional state is calm. These pieces should be larger than the
    holes so that they do not leak out as the water did. Now we have
    something to think about!

    The Point: If a student can't remember or think clearly—often the
    result of test anxiety—it's not because he or she isn't smart. It is prob-
    ably because his or her emotions are forcing the limbic system to
    dump all the information before he or she has a chance to process it.

3. **The Fact**: The brain has different sections for different purposes.

   The Visual: A good way to familiarize students of any age with the various parts and functions of the brain is to use Play-Doh to represent the three major sections—the brain stem (one color), wrapped in the limbic system (another color), wrapped in the cortex (another color). While students are working with each piece, the teacher explains the function of each section. Next, the students cut their Play-Doh brains in half and teach each other the functions and importance of each section. (For a variation on this exercise, visit www.lessonplanspage.com/ScienceArtMakeAPlayDohBrain5.htm.)

   Another visual has students hold their two fists together to show the two hemispheres of the brain. Pass around a grapefruit and a three-pound head of cabbage. The grapefruit is the approximate size of the adult brain and the cabbage is the approximate weight. Also pass around a pillowcase representing the neocortex, which fits over the brain. It gets all its wrinkles from having to fit inside the skull. This is where our dreams, our imagination, and our creativity begin.

   The Point: The brain is not just an abstract concept but a physical entity that is composed of sections that have specific purposes.

Reinforce Understanding of the Brain

Try out the following tactics from the book *What Is It About Me You Can't Teach?* by Eleanor Renée Rodriguez and James Bellanca (2007) to reinforce your students' newfound understandings about their brains and their abilities:

- Elimination of labels and categories that tell students they cannot change
- Increased respect for individual talents, and discouragement of comparisons among students
- Elimination of put-downs, slurs, and personal attacks
- Promotion of student self-evaluation and reflection
- Reduction of self-defeating behavior and language
- Development of an understanding of change within each student
- Use of personal standards and goals to help students guide their changes
- Increased monitoring of self through progress charts and portfolios
- Provision of helpful feedback
- Development of self-reporting parent conferences (p. 201)

Many of these suggestions for instilling healthy brain-based attitudes refer to your development as well as that of your students. When you execute these behaviors, you will find that your students will do the same; your attitudes will dictate those of your class—for example, as you consistently refuse to make comparisons between students, soon students will pick up on this attitude and refrain from doing this themselves.

Offer Opportunities for Movement

Movement during class has a multitude of positive repercussions in engaging students and inspiring upbeat attitudes toward class work. Movement focuses attention more directly on the learning, allows students to physically express their feelings toward the subject matter, and satisfies their need for socialization—generating attitudes of cooperation, self-expression, and delight in most students. The following are simple ways students can move more frequently within the classroom:

- Students stand when delivering an answer.

- Instead of passing up homework, each student gets up and places his or her paper in the designated place. (This also allows you to see who did the work.)

- If there are two sides to an issue, students stand on the side they agree with.

- Instead of the teacher copying what students say on the board, students write their comments on sticky notes and attach them to the headings on the board.

- Students move their desks to make a pair or small group.

- Students fill out a Share Sheet (page 44), gathering information from and giving information to others in the room on a specific topic. (This is also a great way to see what students already know about a topic.)

- Students are given an alternate seating arrangement. Use this arrangement periodically and call, "Change seats!" when starting a new topic during the class period.

- Groups stand to discuss a question or do a group activity.

- Students form a circle to discuss a story or topic, adding "yes, and" to the beginning of each statement so that they connect the comment of the previous student to their own ideas.

- Students in the even rows move to ask a couple of students in the odd rows to proofread their work. Later, the odd rows move and the even rows stay in their chairs.

Reflection on Attitudes

We change our attitudes naturally as we move through life. Can you remember any of the attitudes you had toward school or yourself that changed as you matured? Which were the most influential in later decisions such as to continue in school, to be a teacher, to be a constant learner? Can you point to any person or book that was responsible for any of your changes in attitude? How will you use attitude to engage and motivate your students?

_____

_____

_____

_____

_____

_____

_____

_____

_____

_____

_____

_____

_____

One new strategy you might try out this week:

_____

Bloom's Taxonomy Verbs

Remembering	count, define, describe, draw, enumerate, find, identify, label, list, match, name, quote, read, recall, recite, record, reproduce, select, sequence, state, tell, view, write
Understanding	classify, cite, conclude, convert, describe, discuss, estimate, explain, generalize, give examples, illustrate, interpret, locate, make sense of, paraphrase, predict, report, restate, review, summarize, trace, understand
Applying	act, administer, articulate, assess, change, chart, choose, collect, compute, construct, contribute, control, demonstrate, determine, develop, discover, dramatize, draw, establish, extend, imitate, implement, interview, include, inform, instruct, paint, participate, predict, prepare, produce, provide, relate, report, select, show, solve, transfer, use, utilize
Analyzing	break down, characterize, classify, compare, contrast, correlate, debate, deduce, diagram, differentiate, discriminate, distinguish, examine, focus, illustrate, infer, limit, outline, point out, prioritize, recognize, research, relate, separate, subdivide
Evaluating	appraise, argue, assess, choose, compare and contrast, conclude, criticize, critique, decide, defend, evaluate, interpret, judge, justify, predict, prioritize, prove, rank, rate, reframe, select, support
Creating	adapt, anticipate, categorize, collaborate, combine, communicate, compile, compose, construct, create, design, develop, devise, express, facilitate, formulate, generate, incorporate, individualize, initiate, integrate, invent, make up, model, modify, negotiate, organize, perform, plan, pretend, produce, propose, rearrange, reconstruct, revise, rewrite, structure, substitute, validate

Cultural Awareness

This chapter is the work of Bonnie Davis, PhD, who has written and spoken extensively about culture, equity, and race. Her expertise in this area provides depth and insight into the topic of cultural relevancy and its connection to student engagement.

First Thoughts on Cultural Awareness

Think about what you know about culturally relevant student engagement. How does this knowledge influence your interaction with your students?

_____

_____

_____

_____

_____

_____

_____

_____

_____

_____

_____

_____

Notes From the Field

The following begins this chapter's story of a class of high school students facing their fears to delve into—and thus understand—the various cultures of their school.

> We were all scared. It was the first week of high school, the first week for my fresh-man students, and the first week for me, their teacher. Some students lived within the geographic boundaries of the school district; others were bussed in, part of a "voluntary desegregation" program. But we were all scared. None of us had the guidebook we needed to know what to do, to learn what we didn't know we didn't know. As we introduced ourselves to the class that first day, we decided we needed our own guidebook to the high school. Not the dry impersonal guidebook the school provided; no, we needed to construct our own guidebook and make it per-sonal to our needs: who we were, why we were there, what we were interested in knowing, and where we were going to find what we needed to know. Out of our opening-day conversation came our first lesson, our first high school English proj-ect: we created a guidebook to high school. We made it relevant to us. We, both teacher and students, were engaged!

The Discussion

Each of us views the world through a unique lens that has been created by the many facets of our lives, much like a pair of glasses that allows us to see the world differently from every other person who inhabits it. This world view comprises our heredity, environment, and previous experiences. A culture is the total of everything an individual learns by growing up in a particular con-text, resulting in a set of expectations for appropriate behavior in seemingly similar contexts. Culture provides us with an internal set of hidden rules, those unspoken codes of cultural groups that maintain the status quo of the culture.

Your culture is the lens through which you view the world. By better under-standing your own cultural lens, you can better understand the cultures of the students in your classroom. Students do not check their cultures at the door when they enter your classroom. Instead, they engage with your instruction through their cultural lenses, creating an additional facet of instruction about which you must be aware. How do you gain this awareness? By taking a jour-ney of cultural proficiency to learn what you don't know you don't know in order to offer students culturally relevant pedagogy that results in culturally rel-evant student engagement (Davis, 2006).

We weave in and out of several cultures throughout the day: high school cul-ture, sports culture, gender culture, school culture, student group culture, teacher culture, racial culture, ethnic culture, and so forth. To become proficient in each of these, we need to widen our understanding of culture (Lindsey, Robins, & Terrell, 2003). With this broader understanding, we can capitalize on the many cultures in our classrooms to engage students in culturally relevant instruction.

You can't know everything there is to know about all the cultures in the world; however, you can study the cultures of the students who inhabit your classroom. If you planned to teach in Paris next summer, would you want to learn something about Parisians before the trip? Of course. Yet how often do teachers learn about the cultures of the students sitting in front of them with the same energy and intent they might employ if they were going to teach abroad? The more you learn about the students you teach, the more equipped you are to navigate the different hidden cultural rules by which they operate. When you learn your students' hidden cultural expectations and share yours, you build bridges to understanding and create culturally relevant student engagement.

The Guidebook Project

The guidebook project offered students the opportunity to determine the big picture of their high school experience and to learn about the everyday ins and outs that would help them to navigate fluidly the four-year journey they were about to begin. What did this look like?

1.   Students selected areas they were interested in and identified at least one adult associated with that area.

2.   Students generated a timeline, guidelines for the work, and a rubric.

3.   Students were able to use class time to do much of the work, thus eliminating a disparity of access for some students.

4.   Students knew they had to draft and revise their work as many times as it took to get it to publication quality, and for this extensive work, they would begin their school year in this class with an A.

5.   Students did the work. They typed their chapters, revised, and rewrote for final publication. They created the table of contents, the art on the cover, and all other parts of the publication.

6.   Students knew that their work would result in the publication of a guidebook to share with their peers.

7.   Students each received a guidebook as well as points for doing the assignment.

8.   The unit ended with a celebration, and each student rightfully experienced pride because the guidebook reflected hard, rigorous work and was a proud testament to all the students had done.

In beginning the year with a guidebook to the high school—in many ways, a recipe for success in navigating a new and challenging environment—these students used their own interests, knowledge base, and cultural capital to become fully engaged in the work. *Cultural capital* is described as the skills and knowledge the students have acquired from their personal backgrounds, the *who* of who these students are. Starting the school year with an assignment that embraced the cultural capital of the students made this project culturally relevant and engaging.

In addition, I, their teacher, was new both to the students and the school, and I learned as much as the students did. Not only did I learn much-needed factual knowledge about my new teaching environment, but I also learned much about each of the students. As I talked with students about their chapters for the guidebook, I came to know each on a personal level in a way that standing and delivering content from the front of the room would not have allowed. The project also gave me an opportunity to collect data and observe the learning styles of the students: which students worked best alone, which students needed others for support, which students jumped right into the work, which students needed more discussion and explanation before beginning, which students depended upon relationships with others to spur them on, and which students tended to be concrete and sequential, needing to do things in an orderly sequence. The information I collected created the foundation for the cultural knowledge I would continue to gain about my students throughout the year.

This project offered time for me to speak with the students. As the introduction to this book states, "where, when, what, and how much we speak with students are all part of the relationship mechanism that sets the groundwork for student engagement" (page 2). As I talked with the students, I learned personal information about their lives: which students took an hour-plus bus ride in the morning to arrive at school at the same time as the students who walked from across the street and which students had older siblings in the school who had already informed them about the hidden rules, or expected conduct, of this high school, giving them a distinct advantage and comfort level over those who were ignorant of such rules and completely new to the environment.

I gained a better sense of my students' moods and emotions and began to learn what I needed to know in order to best support the individual needs of each student in the classroom. Because I learned about my students by personally interacting with them, relationships developed as we were able to talk one on one, be physically close, read each other's body language, make eye contact, and listen actively to each other. I truly learned the power of what educator Nan Starling says: "Talk less, listen more" (as quoted in Davis, 2008, p. 129).

Because all of the students were new to the school, they were experiencing some similar emotions in the classroom environment, such as embarrassment, trepidation, uncertainty, excitement, need to please, need to take center stage, fear of risk taking, and others. This project allowed me to assess the maturity of the students and to note which students displayed which behaviors early in the school year, thus giving me feedback for constructing future lessons.

I observed interactions as well as distractions as the students actively engaged in the work. All this became data to use for future planning. Rather than asking students about their learning preferences using a boring survey on a sheet of paper, I observed firsthand who my students were and what they needed in order to achieve.

There were other benefits. The guidebook project allowed me to match students with special needs with others for support, and the matching arose organically from the students' own interests. Two boys interested in learning about the art department and its offerings for students worked together. Students with language challenges worked with students fluent in the language. What tied students together were their interests, not artificial designations made by a teacher who did not yet truly know her students. The lesson itself offered the opportunity for students to learn about each other, learn about their school, and build a community of learners that lasted throughout the year—in other words, to create a classroom culture that wove them together into a tapestry of possibilities, regardless of the diversity of their home cultures.

Culturally Relevant Engagement

When students do real work, they are engaged. Boredom is obliterated. It's as simple as that. Culturally relevant engagement means that students engage in classroom work that speaks to them through their cultural lenses and experiences. Often teachers fear what they don't know about the cultures of the students in their classrooms, yet if they would focus first on lesson design that incorporates students' strengths, regardless of their cultures, they would find the work less daunting. It is not as challenging as it may first seem—we are all human beings who share basic needs. One of those needs is to experience a degree of comfort or safety in our surroundings. Creating a guidebook to the high school allowed these students to do just that. They had the ability to choose what area to investigate, and they were guided by my passion and desire to learn the material just as they wanted to learn it. They were creating a map to their high school experience. When students enter a classroom knowing they get to connect their learning to their life experiences, they engage.

How was the guidebook project culturally relevant? It was culturally relevant on many levels. First, it spoke to the culture of the high school in which all would be participating that year. Next, it spoke to the cultures of the students' interest areas. Of course, there is a sports culture. And yes, there is a culture particular to students who join choir, jazz band, and other music classes. And true to life, there is a culture of students interested in technology. So the cultures of the subjects chosen by the students were relevant to those students. The guidebook assignment also spoke to gender culture. Sometimes the areas of choice broke down into cultures of gender such as girls' field hockey and the boys' football team. It also spoke to the culture of student groups. One student investigated the African American Academic Achievers' club; another interviewed and wrote about the journalism club; another learned about and reported on crew (something I was clueless about until I read the student's work); and so on. So the cultures of student groups added another layer of culture to the guidebook. There were others, too, of course, but it's easy to understand how the definitions of culture were expanded through such an assignment.

Students from diverse cultural backgrounds brought their cultural strengths to an assignment that offered them choice, information they desperately wanted, an opportunity to work with peers, freedom of physical movement, time to do the work within the classroom setting, and a final product to be celebrated and shared with others.

Possible Variations

The power of this guidebook project is multifaceted. Because I was learning with the students, I modeled the best of learning: passion for the subject matter, mistakes made during the process of learning, concrete goal-oriented success, and voicing a daily connection to the students' lives. Granted, this project fits easily into the English curriculum, but how does one translate this to other content areas? In other areas, it might look different, yet the reasons for and benefits of implementing a project such as this at the beginning of a school year remain the same.

In other content areas, one might use the principles of this project to learn about student currencies (discussed later in this chapter), behaviors, and strengths during the opening days of the school year. Students can design a guidebook, however abbreviated, for each of their content areas. This "Guide to Math" or "Guide to Social Studies" or guide for any other content area would include the skills needed to succeed in that content area as well as the schema for the content, the teacher's expectations for the students, and other pertinent information to ensure that students know the hidden rules of that class.

Teaching the hidden rules and the skills needed to perform in a content area is one way to make the learning culturally relevant to students' lives. Yet some teachers don't do that; they assume that students understand the schema of the discipline and their expectations for the classroom. It is up to all teachers to teach students what they don't know they don't know about being successful in every classroom and every content area. This includes classroom behavior expectations, skills needed to achieve in the subject matter, and concepts of the content. And if students learn that schema and develop the skills to interact with it, they are then more likely to be engaged without the stress that can put a stranglehold on their cognitive processes.

Student Currencies

In *Never Work Harder Than Your Students and Other Principles of Great Teaching*, Robyn R. Jackson (2009) writes that "any behavior that students use to acquire the knowledge and skills important to your class functions as currency" (p. 7). Students used the following behaviors, or currencies, in the course of the guidebook project: they worked with their peers; they designed and created both the interview questions and the rubrics for the project; they talked with and interviewed adults in the building in areas of interest; and they used the literacy skills of reading, writing, speaking, and listening. I had the opportunity to observe which student currencies were strengths and which needed more support.

Teaching students how to learn in each of our content areas is culturally relevant teaching. As Jackson (2009) asks, "Can you really effectively get to know all 20–35 students in your classroom or make a personal connection with each one fast enough or deeply enough to help each student find a way to access the curriculum?" (p. 8). Certainly not on the first day nor even during the first weeks of a school year. Therefore, teachers must engage students through lesson design that is culturally relevant to the currency they bring to the classroom. Learning where your students are and what strengths they bring to the classroom gives you the platform on which to build the learning.

Steps Toward Solutions

> *No significant learning occurs without a significant relationship.*
>
> —James Comer

For many teachers, understanding the ethnic and racial cultures of their students who do not look like them poses challenges. Taking a journey to learn cultural proficiency lays the groundwork for continued growth. Professional learning communities or informal groups of staff can embark upon book studies to build background knowledge and foster new understandings. Consider reading books that investigate and illuminate cultural understanding, such as *How to Teach Students Who Don't Look Like You: Culturally Relevant Teaching Strategies* (Davis, 2006), *Courageous Conversations About Race: A Field Guide for Achieving Equity in Schools* (Singleton & Linton, 2006), and *The Biracial and Multiracial Student Experience: A Journey to Racial Literacy* (Davis, 2009).

Get to Know Your Students

Learn who your students are as individuals first, not as members of a group. Greet students at the door each day, call on students by their names, and use students' names during lessons. During the first days of a new school year, have students share their favorite things with the class and write personal narratives or poems about themselves. Take time to speak individually with each student at some point during the first days of school.

Connect the Learning to Real Life

For each lesson, purposely write in how you will connect the teaching to the personal lives of the students. For example, if you are a Spanish teacher and teaching students the parts of the face, you might break up the instruction and ask each student, "What kind of toothpaste do you use?" By beginning with one student and having each student respond in turn, you can provide the class with a break in the instruction, or a brain break, as well as share commonalities among the students, which builds a feeling of cohesiveness or community in the classroom. Students also usually engage in this kind of activity since it includes their peers. Ask students how they might connect the learning with their lives. Have them brainstorm and come up with the connections.

Be a Learner

Be a learner *with* your students. Use each lesson design as an opportunity to learn what you don't know by reading new books, surfing for new information, and talking to experts and colleagues. Share with your students that you don't know everything, but you're willing to learn with them. Be passionate about your curiosity for learning—it is infectious.

Talk about the book you are reading with your students. Post your yearly reading list above the light switch in your classroom. Add each new book you read, rate it for your students on a scale of 1 to 10, and list its appropriate reading level. Invite students to post their reading lists on the walls of your classroom.

Utilize Emotions

Don't fear dealing with the emotions of your students. Instead, construct opportunities, such as student interviews and small- and whole-group discussions, for students to discuss their feelings. Use feelings as a way to begin a conversation about the text the class is reading and studying. Have students discuss how they might enter the text as a character. What would their character look and sound like? What would their character do to advance or change the plot? Have them write their responses for a different kind of creative essay about the text.

Continue the Cultural Journey

Continue your journey to cultural proficiency by learning about your students' ethnic and racial heritages and identities. Incorporate students' cultural capital by allowing students to be the experts whenever possible during the instruction. Consider where your students live and play and purposely include their home cultures in your lessons. Commit to reading a fictional book each quarter that reflects a segment of your students' cultures. Find authors who reflect the cultures of the students in your classroom. Post their pictures on the walls, and bring their stories into the classroom.

Continue learning about your cultural lens and how it daily impacts your classroom instruction and relationships with students. Push yourself outside your comfort zone by attending unfamiliar cultural events. Keep a journal detailing your experiences as you continue your cultural journey.

Reflection on Cultural Awareness

Discuss several ways in which you might make your classroom instruction and lessons culturally relevant to better engage and motivate your students.

_____

_____

_____

_____

_____

_____

_____

_____

_____

_____

_____

_____

_____

_____

_____

_____

_____

One new strategy you might try out this week:

_____

Expectations

This chapter will discuss what we expect when we look at our students, why we form these expectations, and what we can do to avoid false or low expectations about our students' abilities. The self-fulfilling prophesy theory can have dramatic effects on our actions and expectations; therefore, we will take a look at how this affects the way we think and consequently act in our classes.

First Thoughts on Expectations

In this chapter, we look at what we expect of ourselves and of our students. Studies have shown that no matter what the district or school has set in place in its curriculum and standards, it is the expectations of the teacher that often drive the achievement level of the students (Boehlert, 2005). Think about an experience with a person who gave you the impression you were more than capable of performing at a high level. Then think about a person whose attitude made you doubt your ability and consequently your performance.

_____

_____

_____

_____

_____

_____

_____

_____

Notes From the Field

The following is a poetic vignette about a student I've taught.

Girl in Black With Raspberry Hair

Smudged eye makeup
black fingertips
big heavy boots and mesh stockings.
Spiky hair
with a spray-painted look
of raspberry and lemon.
Marissa.
Someone's tiny baby once
in pink ribbons
and dainty duck-print dresses.
What baby steps
brought her eventually
to become
the young lady
in my back row
with a chain-like necklace
and mask-like face?
The truth is
she's dazzlingly brilliant
and as the days go by
I begin to see
the jewel of a girl
glow
in wave upon wave
of shimmering color
from the soul up and out
through the black habit
of her choosing—
No. Marissa can't hide
the miracle of herself
from me—
Not for long.

The Discussion

As humans, we are often manipulated by the insidious workings of our unconscious minds when it comes to making judgments about others' intelligence, ability levels, motivations, and capacities for achievement. We are all subject to the urge to stereotype those we meet. Our brains are constantly creating patterns and attempting to place new stimuli within these patterns.

So when a teacher sees Marissa for the first time, that teacher's past experience with others who dress like Marissa and assume the same body language activates the checklist of what behaviors, attitudes, and level of classroom involvement to expect. What we expect to find in Marissa is often what we end up finding regardless of what she has to offer or how objective we think we are. We tend to get the behavior that we expect to receive. This phenomenon has been labeled as a self-fulfilling prophecy or the Pygmalion effect. Robert Rosenthal, a professor of social psychology at Harvard, broke down this cycle this way: we first form expectations of students; we communicate these expectations through our body language or direct speech and actions; students then respond to these cues by changing their behaviors to match them; and the result is that the expectations we first formed come true (Rosenthal, 1968).

Classroom Expectations

There are certain social and behavioral competencies that teachers expect students to have as they enter the classroom. Most revolve around a student's ability to listen attentively, do work correctly, follow directions, and control his or her temper. These expectations can often be unclear to students. Although it would seem that these behaviors are pretty much ingrained in children from preschool, they aren't. For example, the body language of one attentive student might vary from the body language of another attentive student. And what the teacher considers to be the body language of an attentive student might be something entirely different. Even though the two students are paying attention, the teacher doesn't believe this is true and sets lower expectations for their behavior in the classroom. Cultural differences, in particular, might send messages that teachers misinterpret (Gay, 2000).

Researchers have found that teachers rate cooperation and self-control skills as more important for success in school than assertion skills. We tend to expect a passive, get-along behavior while giving lip service to our desire for students to exhibit self-expression and authenticity (Lynne, Lane, Pierson, & Givner, 2003).

Marissa, because of her style of dress, at first glance appears to be in a state of rebellion against the basic social expectations held by most teachers. Students like Marissa might dress and attempt to appear a part of the gothic subculture because they have experienced difficulties at school or at home and feel alienated. Often their appearance mirrors those feelings and is how they choose to express themselves (Evans & Ardill, 1999). Teachers may see Marissa's exterior and make a judgment about what they can expect from her as a student: disagreeable, lacking motivation or willingness to participate, not a team player, lacking intelligent curiosity, rebellious, uncooperative.

We all have deeply embedded reactions to certain types of people, causing us to make quick decisions on what we perceive to be their personalities, potentials, and intelligence levels. These reactions float within us and often surface automatically. We can't change that very easily. However, when we accept these judgments as truth and act upon them, we fall short of that tolerant, all-accepting, open attitude we all hope characterizes our behavior in the classroom. Knowledge of what surface characteristics cause us to jump to premature conclusions is the best tool at our disposal to counteract our own biases and unconsciously held prejudices.

The basis for holding high expectations for all children under our care is respect for them as individuals and the belief in their unlimited range of possibility as learners. This demands slaying our personal dragons of prejudgment. Prejudgment tendencies could result from any of the cultural, religious, political, racial, gender, or socioeconomic differences that exist between teacher and student. According to the 2009 *MetLife Survey of the American Teacher*,

> Despite the widespread belief in the importance of high expectations for all and that teachers display this in the classroom, teachers' own reports demonstrate that high expectations exist for many or some students, but not for all. Only 36% of teachers and 51% of principals believe that all of their students have the ability to succeed academically. (MetLife, p. 7)

Meet Justin

Parent-teacher conferences always seem to come so early in the school year. This particular year's scheduled meetings were no exception. Our school's system blocked out an evening session from 5 p.m. to 8 p.m. and a morning session the next day from 8 a.m. to noon. All parents were welcome to come in or sit outside the classrooms and wait for their turn to visit with their child's teachers. We never knew who would show up. Since our school was experiencing a great deal of growth, it seemed there was never enough room for the new influx of students we received every fall. Our class rosters bulged with around thirty-five names per each of our six classes. Add the early time of the school year to the size of our student load, and it is easy to understand how mix-ups like the following incident are possible.

A lady who appeared a bit haggard entered my classroom and took a chair next to my desk. In a soft-spoken voice, she asked how her son Justin was doing in my sophomore English writing class. I asked her what hour he was in since I seemed to have been blessed with a bumper crop of boys with this name. My third hour. I checked my seating chart and mentally tried to picture this group of fifteen-year-olds.

ME	Yes! Oh, Justin. He's doing fine. He sits right over there in the second row.
MOTHER	He is? That's remarkable. I thought that he would find a writing class difficult.
ME	I'm used to boys being a little more than worried about what they'll have to do to live through a semester of writing. I ease them into it before they even realize what's happening to them! I love the challenge.
MOTHER	So Justin isn't giving you trouble and is doing his work?
ME	Yes, he's doing his work, and no, he's not being any trouble.
MOTHER	This is the first parent-teacher conference since Justin was in third grade that actually had something positive to report about his behavior and work. I'm amazed.
ME	Well, he's probably maturing. He's got a B so far and is delightful to have in class.
MOTHER	You can't understand just how much this means to me. Whatever you are doing must be working. Thank you. Keep me informed if this changes in any way. I always try to keep on top of things when it comes to my youngest.

The next day, the third-hour class walked into the room, and Justin sat down— next to the chair I had thought was his. As the other students took their seats, it dawned on me that the boy I had spoken about was Jason W., not Justin W., who sat at the desk next to him. Oh my. Justin came up to me.

JUSTIN	What did you tell my mom? Why did you tell her I was doing good in here and was getting a B? I told her there must have been a mistake.
ME	I screwed up! I got you mixed up with Jason who sits next to you. I told her you were great, a delight to have in class, a strong B student. I told her you had probably matured.

JUSTIN	Well, that's not true. You've got to tell her you were wrong.
ME	No way! No ever-loving way will I do that! You should have seen your mother's face when I started describing how I saw you in my class. She looked at me like I was an angel or something. No way are we going to break her heart and tell her I was wrong.
JUSTIN	Then what are we going to do? Are you just going to give me a B?
ME	Justin, you are going to earn that B this semester, and you are not going to tell your mother what I did.
JUSTIN	I can't do that! I've never gotten over a C in anything. I can't get a B, especially in a writing class!
ME	You're wrong. . . . You and I are going to see to it that you *do* earn that grade. If I have to haunt you *every* time a paper is due, find you at lunchtime to remind you, meet you at the bus, seek you out in study hall, you are going to get all your work in, and you are going to get that work in well done! You are not going to embarrass me or disappoint your mother by doing anything less.
JUSTIN	OK, I'll keep your secret, and we'll see. I'd rather do the work than have you sit next to me during lunch.
ME	And you'll be a delight to have in class too, right?
JUSTIN	Now that's pushing it.

So what happened? Justin earned his B and found it hysterically funny the whole time. He was a poster boy for underachievers anonymous. He never considered that applying himself to his class work might not be as painful a deal as he had thought. In fact, he began to apply himself in his other classes as well. When report cards came out, he dropped by my class to show me how he had raised his grade point average and his effort grades. He asked me if it was now OK to tell his mother about my mistake. I told him, "No. She doesn't need to know that. Leave her blissfully ignorant of the whole thing."

During the next two years before Justin graduated, he would periodically pop his head into the room and ask, "Now? Can I tell her now?" and I would answer, "No, not yet!" We kept this up with the smiles and laughter of two people who shared an inside joke. At graduation, Justin, his mother, and I talked, and Justin and I came clean.

Eye Contact Influences Expectations

Without even realizing it, we may be communicating our expectations of students through our body language. Professor Albert Mehrabian, of the University of California, Los Angeles (UCLA), is credited as the originator of the 7–38–55 rule of communication that states that our communication is 7 percent words, 38 percent tonality, and 55 percent physiology (Mehrabian, 1971). Our whole bodies communicate to others—especially to children.

One such area is that of eye contact and the possible misinterpretations that can affect our expectations for student achievement. White, native English-speaking teachers expect their students to make eye contact when listening and yet not necessarily make eye contact when replying. This pattern is reversed in some nonwhite cultures. Teachers can misinterpret this lack of eye contact while listening and consequently come to the conclusion that the student is not interested, is thinking about other things, lacks the ability to pay attention, is uncooperative, or is engaging in off-task behaviors (Gay, 2000). What could be rudeness or a sign of disrespect in one culture could easily be construed as attentiveness and interest in another. If a student exhibits a great deal of eye contact, teachers tend to consider this a sign of attentiveness and intelligence, leading to a more positive attitude toward that child's ability and capacity and to higher expectations (Miller, 2005).

Research, such as that of Harris Cooper concerning a teacher's habits of eye contact, can go a long way to help teachers be more observant of the messages they are sending unwittingly. Cooper found that teachers' eye contact fosters a warmer, "socioemotional" connection with the students whom they believe are "bright." They look into the eyes of these students longer, nod their heads in approval more often, and lean toward them when speaking. He also found that when teachers were told that some of their students who were originally considered "slow" were actually more intelligent, they changed their behavior almost immediately and began giving those students the benefit of the warmth and extended eye contact that the "brights" were getting. This change in the teachers' behavior caused the students who were originally considered "slow" to participate more often and be more attentive (Cooper, 1979). This was definitely the situation with Justin.

If the unintentional misidentification had never occurred, Justin probably would never have been given the eye contact and affirmation concerning his work that he received that semester. His rise in achievement would not have been my normal expectation for him considering his prior academic background. I might have even thought myself a success if he had earned a C since he usually had all Ds on his report card.

There are many Justins in our classes who easily slip between the cracks of our higher expectations because they have not been given the opportunity or attention necessary to experience success in such a long time that they have no idea they are capable of it now. Again, it is the respect for children as individuals and the belief in their unlimited range of possibility as learners that is the key to lifting our level of expectation for their success. Not only did Justin see himself as incapable of earning a B, I didn't really see him as capable of that, either—at least not until we decided we were going to make sure we succeeded.

Expectations and Intellectual Rigor

Teachers, for a variety of reasons, sometimes feel that they are incapable of raising their students' achievement—that they personally lack the skills, strategies, energy, and motivation to move children from low achievement to high achievement. When this feeling sets in, teachers will often act in one of two ways: Some will set the goals for student achievement so high that it is impossible to reach them. Then they will explain how they are indeed providing intellectual rigor, but the students are incompetent and unwilling to reach those goals. Others will lower the bar so far down that there is no challenge, no rigor. They do this under the misconception that they have to keep the students safe from failure and avoid the tension of pushing them out of their comfort zones. These are the teachers who can be heard saying, "Our students need more order and structure. Our students won't know how to behave if we put them in groups or try to hold a discussion or work on projects." They think they are helping their students by shielding them from challenges they might not be able to meet. Students seldom have higher expectations for themselves than those in charge have for them. These students' potentials are indeed being killed by a hollow semblance of kindness and sympathy.

An example of this misplaced kindness was witnessed by Kylene Beers, president of the National Council of Teachers of English, while visiting a large urban high school. Students were not allowed to leave their seats—not for discussion or work at the board, not for anything. *These students* need discipline, need structure, can't handle the freedom that other students can, she was told. Beers (2009)

> saw [teachers] distribute photocopied packets that reduced complex topics such as the Holocaust to a series of questions requiring only literal thinking and written answers in complete sentences, black ink only. [She] asked teachers if they thought classroom discussions might be helpful. All answered no, not for their students. (p. 2)

The expectations for these students were to learn to follow rules, memorize facts, and stay in their seats. In her report, *The Genteel Unteaching of America's Poor*, Beers (2009) quotes a science teacher:

> Some kids can handle the higher-level thinking discussions you might see in other schools, but not the kids here; the kids here haven't had anyone show them how to act, so we do. We demand they sit still and answer questions, and they learn how to do that. We demand that they memorize information. (p. 2)

In many similar schools, writing lessons are reduced to reciting grammar rules, circling nouns or verbs, and copying from books rather than thinking and creating original texts. In many classrooms, teachers are overly concerned about form at the expense of content. When this is the case, students have little opportunity to experience writing as a thinking tool, a tool for learning and self-expression, as it is meant to be.

What their teachers take to be rigor, students in these schools experience as drudgery. No wonder they drop out as soon as they are legally able. Low expectations strip children of the opportunity to think, be challenged, make choices, and experience the joy of learning, making them victims of systematic bigotry and prejudice. Beers' (2009) stark observation is summarized best when she states: "In the end, we are left with an education of America's poor that cannot be seen as anything more than a segregation by intellectual rigor, something every bit as shameful and harmful as segregation by color" (p. 3).

Expectations of Teachers

The expectations that teachers have for student behavior and achievement are not the only expectations that teachers must consider. Students have expectations of what teachers should be like; parents, administrators, and fellow faculty members have expectations of how teachers should conduct themselves and their classes. A wise teacher will be sure to find out what the community's and school's expectations are when taking a new job. Such expectations cover many areas, such as the use or abuse of social networks, written and unwritten dress codes, the gray areas of teacher-student relationships, keeping the secretaries and custodians happy, and classroom evaluations.

Many of the interactions and behaviors outside of the classroom walls involve living up to expectations that others hold for teachers. Discussing what these expectations are in one's current situation is an exercise that is well worth the time and energy.

Steps Toward Solutions

It seems to me, engagement is a few things. The first is to believe that every kid can—and wants to—learn. The desire to get better at stuff and to unravel mysteries is part of being human. The second is to connect what kids learn to the big picture. In our quest for reading, writing, and arithmetic, we sometimes lose sight of the fourth R: relevance. Finally, while people do have different abilities, it's clear that persistence, practice, great coaching, and high expectations are more important than innate talent. That makes a teacher's job even more important than we already know it is.

—Daniel Pink

The 2009 *MetLife Survey of the American Teacher* reported some rather disturbing statistics: although 86 percent of teachers feel that their expectations are important to student performance, only 36 percent of teachers and 51 percent of principals believe that the students they work with have the ability to arrive at academic success (MetLife, 2009). In this section, we will work on setting high expectations for all of our students by examining our own expectations of others and considering elements that could influence how we judge our students' abilities.

Foster High Expectations

We often create unconscious prejudices against those who are least like us—in culture, race, personality, socioeconomic status, and so on—and think these children are unlikely to perform as well as those children who are similar to us. Because of this propensity to harbor low expectations for such children, I suggest that you determine which struggling student would be the least likely to be your child, and mentally "adopt" him or her for the school year. Decide that this child—like Justin—will succeed and you will pull out all the stops to see that he or she does. Don't tell the child what you are doing, of course. If you succeed with this child, other children will benefit from this experience because you will have developed a sensitivity that affects all other such children. You will prove to yourself that under the right circumstances, all children can learn!

A variation on this exercise is to decide that a child in your class is the son or daughter of a board member, principal, or district superintendent. Again, choose a child that you are tempted to think negatively about, one who seems to irritate or exasperate you more than the others in the class. Note in what ways you act differently toward this student. Do you hold your tongue at times? Are you sure to plan lessons that are complete and interesting? Do you give those students the best you have to offer by way of attention and help? This is an effective exercise when you are vaguely aware that you may be marginalizing a student under your care.

Meet Students' Expectations

Before working with a faculty, a presenter was warned by the contact person that if she seemed to be boring the faculty or offering irrelevant material, the principal would stop her and shut down the workshop right then and there. This was a statement of expectations with a pretty stiff penalty if not met; we demand that our own teachers not bore us with monotone lectures, long bouts of passive inactivity, and dull presentations. What if our students had the same power to set expectations and object to or demand better of us? With this in mind, read the list of what is necessary to engage teacher participants in workshops (pages 151–152). Then consider this to be a list of items necessary to engage students in class day after day. Gather a group of colleagues, pass out this list (visit **go.solution-tree.com/instruction** to download the reproducibles in this book), and ask each to complete the following exercise:

1. Mark the list from most important (1) to least important (26).
2. Explain why you ranked the top three items as most important.
3. Explain why you ranked the last three items as least important.
4. Discuss the items each person chose as his or her top and bottom items.
5. If you are working in a group, come to a consensus on which items students would find most important.

Be Aware of Factors That Influence Your Expectations

Since expectations are often formed on the first days of class, students can begin the year at a disadvantage or an advantage, depending on our first impressions. Impressions and expectations are constructed so deep in our psyche without our conscious awareness that it is important to continually question and contain our first impulses to label and judge students on externals. In other words, the more aware we are of our natural tendency to form expectations on scanty data, the more likely we will be to hold high expectations for all children. To heighten your awareness, fill out the Factors That Influence Expectations worksheet (pages 153–154).

Reflection on Expectations

What new information did you glean from this chapter? Explain how
this information might be incorporated into your teaching. How can you
use expectations to engage and motivate your students? What area of
expectations do you feel you need to concentrate on more intensely: your
expectations for yourself as a teacher or your expectations for a certain
population of your class? Write about this, and formulate a plan to begin
addressing this issue.

_____

_____

_____

_____

_____

_____

_____

_____

_____

_____

_____

_____

_____

_____

One new strategy you might try out this week:

_____

What's Necessary to Engage Teachers in Workshops

Planning for the workshop

____ Know your audience and adapt the material to their interests and needs.

____ Plan to have the participants do the strategy you are teaching (avoid "sit and get" behaviors).

____ Don't try to cover too much material; rather, select a few big concepts to explore in a variety of ways.

____ Schedule frequent opportunities for participants to stop, summarize, and reflect using a "tell your neighbor what you just heard" strategy.

____ Vary the methods of presenting information as often as possible: PowerPoints, videos, speaking, handouts, group work, chart making, and so forth.

____ Provide time at the end of the workshop for a reflective evaluation to allow the audience to determine whether their goals were met and to afford you individual feedback on what areas were seen as important or unnecessary.

Gathering materials

____ Have actual student models of lessons, projects, and papers to serve as samples.

____ Use markers, chart paper, colored paper, props, or interactive handouts for participant input.

____ Have all materials and electronic equipment ready and tested before the workshop begins.

____ If you use a PowerPoint presentation, don't fill it with dense written material, don't read it to the audience, and don't force them to copy your material. Provide handouts if you feel this material is necessary for them to have.

Beginning the workshop

____ Before the workshop, spend your time talking and making connections with the participants as they come in and settle down.

____ Set goals; involve participants in setting group norms, plus their own personal goals for the session.

Page 1 of 2

Working the room

____ Set up the room so everyone can easily see and hear, so everyone will feel included.

____ Move around the group; don't stand in one place very long, and don't speak from only one area of the room if possible.

____ Have participants move around, sharing information and/or preparing and giving demonstrations.

____ Have participants work with varied groups throughout the session—partners, four to five people, whole group, alone.

Delivering content

____ Use a variety of activities; don't stay on one piece too long.

____ Balance theory and practical suggestions so everyone has something concrete they can immediately try out in their classrooms.

____ Use novelty, nonlinguistic methods, and choice to present difficult concepts.

____ Only spend time on relevant, meaningful material and activities that are applicable to your primary goals.

During the workshop

____ Vary your voice, and use gestures to punctuate your language.

____ Monitor participants' body language for understanding and engagement; alter your presentation if you feel it is not paced correctly for the group.

____ Use humor by having participants act out prepared skits or demonstrations.

____ Give breaks for personal needs.

____ Allow time for questions, which are opportunities to relate the information to participants' specific situations.

____ Give volunteers positive feedback on their remarks or contributions.

Factors That Influence Expectations

Following is a list of factors that may influence the expectations you have for students. Put a check mark in front of those that apply to you. Add a few more to the list.

1 ☐ Student is an English learner.

2 ☐ Student is on the free or reduced lunch program.

3 ☐ Student's dress or hairstyle is eccentric.

4 ☐ Student's clothing is dirty and smells.

5 ☐ Student is openly gay.

6 ☐ Student does not make eye contact.

7 ☐ Student's language is not conventionally correct.

8 ☐ Student is biracial.

9 ☐ Student is a person of color.

10 ☐ Student is of the Muslim faith.

11 ☐ Student does not belong to any faith.

12 ☐ Student belongs to a faith that requires accommodations in school rules.

13 ☐ Student is openly prejudiced against minorities.

14 ☐ Student's father has multiple tattoos and long hair.

15 ☐ Student's mother is a single parent.

16 ☐ Student is absent frequently.

17 ☐ Student never mixes with others, is a loner.

18 ☐ Student's parents never come to school functions.

19 ☐ Student's parents contest specific curriculum materials as being inappropriate.

20 ☐ Student's behavior is unruly and problematic.

21 ☐ Student has never gotten high grades.

22 ☐ Student constantly questions the teacher's judgment.

Page 1 of 2

You've Got to Reach Them to Teach Them © 2011 Solution Tree Press • solution-tree.com
Visit **go.solution-tree.com/instruction** to download this page.

23 ☐ Student has a physical handicap.

24 ☐ Student has an individual education program (IEP).

25 ☐ Student expresses a distinct dislike for the subject matter.

26 ☐ Student shows signs of learned helplessness.

27 ☐ Student refuses to stand for the Pledge of Allegiance.

28 ☐ Student is pregnant.

29 ☐ Student is frequently the victim of bullies.

30 ☐ Student is periodically homeless.

31 ☐ Student lacks a basic educational foundation.

_____

_____

_____

_____

_____

The Engagement Toolbox

Whenever I begin a workshop for new teachers, I give them the following advice: you will be offered many varied and rich opportunities for professional development during your teaching career, and the mindset you assume when acting on these opportunities will determine how valuable they will be for you. If you can come away with a few new ideas or with a few strategies that you can incorporate in your class instruction, you have had a successful session. Not every idea or strategy will be appropriate for you. Pick those that seem to be a good fit.

I suggest that you read this chapter with much the same mindset. Many tools are highlighted here; pick the ideas and strategies that seem to be a good fit for you and your class.

First Thoughts on the Engagement Toolbox

This chapter covers a wide variety of tools—tangible and abstract—that help the teacher to grab and hold his or her students' attention. What do you keep in your cabinets? An inventory might tell you a lot about your teaching style and your attitude toward multisensory engagement. Sometimes we think we appear one way or another, but our cabinets tell us otherwise. Many of you might not realize just how much you do try to make your lessons more alive and understandable. What is your cabinet telling you about your teaching?

_____

_____

_____

_____

_____

Notes From the Field

Welcome to my prop cabinet.

Inside you will find many treasures. A large bag of ladies' wigs—curly, straight, white, black, brown, short, long—came in handy for many role-playing, script-reading activities throughout the year. My mother's graduation gown from college served as a judge's robe for trial reenactments, complete with a gavel in one of the pockets. Over the years, students left pieces of clothing, costumes they designed to represent different characters in literature, and sheets and wreaths from mythology banquets. I even had a doll dressed up like little Pearl from Hawthorne's *The Scarlet Letter*.

For me, supplies didn't mean pens, sticky notes, and copier paper. Supplies meant numerous sets of markers, highlighters, cans of spray paint, an industrial-size roll of butcher paper, enough colored folders with pockets for each class member, boxes of manila folders, a box of coin envelopes, packages of stickers, and colored masking tape. From after-Halloween sales, I bought large sets of chains, witches' hats, eyeballs, and assorted play weapons. From after-Christmas sales, I bought boxes of table confetti, gift packages, and tiny blank books. Anything cheap and in a set of thirty or more was a find. I had puppets and tiny action figures. I had a couple gross of large balloon sticks and lots of mail-order catalogs. Boxes of Play-Doh filled the bottom shelf. CDs of music were brought in to be played at various times during class. Tiny Slinkys taught students the concept of sentence variation. You get the idea.

Research has shown that students demonstrate improved comprehension when reading texts that they find interesting compared to when they read other types of text (Renninger, Hidi, & Krapp, 1992). With this in mind, I filled file boxes with magazine and newspaper articles for interesting reading in free moments. Bookshelves were filled with books gathered over the years—some donated by students and teachers, others ordered with extra funds from the department budget—that covered a wide scope of interests and reading levels. These books were accessible to all my students at all times. Even students who were no longer in my classes would drop by to borrow these books despite the fact that we had a well-stocked library.

None of this is unusual to the average elementary school teacher. The unusual part of this list of gadgets and fix-it items is that it belonged to a high school teacher. Too many high school teachers don't feel the need to make their material tangible. When it comes to engaging students through manipulatives and an appeal to the five senses, we all can learn from the elementary school world.

The Discussion

Most toolboxes have a variety of items tucked inside: some are serious, high-powered tools for very precise purposes; some are basics; some are gadgets; and some are simply leftovers from fix-it jobs. The engagement toolbox is no different. There are serious, high-powered tools, such as formative assessments, meaning and relevance, and technology. There are basics, such as the application of multiple intelligences and project-based learning. And there are great gadgets and fix-it items, such as cameras and props. All these come into play when we attempt to reach and teach our students.

Take My Picture! Using Your Camera as a Tool

When teachers engage students, they are leading with the students' interests in mind. Nothing seems to stimulate a student's interest, self-esteem, curiosity, or feeling of involvement like a picture of himself or herself in the classroom. The ultimate tool for the classroom teacher is a camera.

Maximize Memory

When posting pictures of students involved in lessons and projects, a teacher is maximizing students' memories. Seeing themselves and those they know working on class content creates a positive emotional response, which reinforces the memory of the event tremendously. Researchers have discovered that ideas are much more likely to be remembered if they are presented as pictures instead of words or pictures paired with words. Psychologists call this picture superiority effect (PSE). If information is presented orally, people remember about 10 percent of the content seventy-two hours later. That figure goes up to 65 percent if you add a picture (Gallo, 2009).

Tapping into PSE is far easier today than ever before. Digital cameras are reasonably priced, can download pictures immediately to a computer, and can even offer video that is clear and easily accessible. The Flip, a small video camera, is probably one of the more user-friendly, reasonably priced cameras, offering high definition and instant playback viewing. The uses for cameras in the classroom are limited only by the imagination of the teacher.

Strengthen Reading Fluency

Building reading fluency is often more difficult with older students. Although the repeated reading of a piece is probably the best way to strengthen reading fluency, it is not likely to be sold to a group of adolescents as easily as it is to elementary children. A great way to embed fluency is to provide a platform for performance. If students are told that they will be filmed while performing—reading parts in a play, choral reading a poem, participating in a readers' theatre—they will rehearse their particular portions of the text. Filming brings out that built-in desire to do well. Since any repetition of written material has the effect of building fluency in reading new material at a later date, this rehearsal is exactly what we want. The presence of the little camera offers just the incentive necessary to get students to practice.

A bonus of filming students in action is the repetition that occurs when you play back the film. If they were demonstrating, discussing, or working with content or procedures that are necessary for them to remember, then watching themselves provides the extra benefit of hearing and seeing the important material again and again.

Filming for Feedback

A filmed debate or discussion can be used as quality material in its own right, not only for an opportunity to repeat. Teachers could prepare a follow-up lesson using the film to share with the class a thoughtful analysis of how students did or did not quite grasp the directions of the activity, what level of questioning students employed, how many students participated with in-depth responses, and eventually how the next time could be improved. This is a perfect feedback tool; students can immediately see what they need to change, repeat, or reject for a better presentation.

Homemade Posters

Posters of school rules, classroom rules, standards, goals, and procedures related to specific content are always found gracing classroom walls. The problem is that mandating that these items be visible doesn't guarantee they are really "visible" in the students' eyes. Students simply don't read posted sheets of densely written material—adults don't either, for that matter. If the information posted is important enough to be looked at over and over again by the students in class, then the teacher needs to do something more than just stick it up on the wall with a border around it or copy the material on colored paper. A way to make sure this material is continuously viewed is to mix in two prime engagement elements: humor and pictures.

When it's time to make the list of class rules and procedures, ask volunteers to role-play students involved in the various procedures. Take cameo shots of these students as they demonstrate the correct or incorrect behavior or both. Have these images blown up to eight-by-eleven-inch full-color pictures. Attach captions describing the rule, infraction, explanation—whatever is most appropriate—and post these. Your rules and regulations now have the attention of the entire class.

Self-Actualization Through Meaning

What is the purpose of schooling—meaning or money?

Meaning here refers to that which brings a sense of deep purpose and a consequent state of bliss to one's life. According to George Land and Beth Jarman (1992), leading experts in how organizations and individuals both embrace and resist change:

> Most of our cultural conditioning tells us we can't do what we love to do. Conventional wisdom says work is work and fun is fun and you can't combine them. Making a living is a serious business. . . . It is estimated that of all the people that go to college only 15 percent ever work in the field of their major. And, within that huge college population, only 2 percent of them will do what they really love to do with their lives. (p. 181)

It seems that money has become the all-encompassing badge of success, leading the top students away from their primary joys, passions, and desires, which would otherwise flow from a commitment to their innate creativeness.

If we assume that success equals money, then we will likely discourage our own children from following their innate gifts and preferences and urge them instead to move into careers that pay well. We are afraid to encourage the artist to pursue art, the child who is skilled in woodworking to go into carpentry, the singer to take her voice seriously—"You'll starve! Or worse yet, I'll have to support you the rest of my life!" We, as educators, often have a deep prejudice against trade schools as opposed to four-year colleges. Some of us don't think that our children should follow their unique skills and talents if those skills and talents don't assure them the prestige of a big salary. Often this same bias bleeds into our classrooms and our interactions with our students.

What is the purpose of schooling? To help children find their purposes in this life by providing opportunities to uncover and expose their purposes, to prepare them to successfully follow those purposes, and to encourage and honor them along the day-to-day journey through curriculum guides and efforts at reaching standards. On determining a person's life purpose, Land and Jarman (1992) write:

> To uncover your own purpose, focus on those unique qualities that describe who you are, and then look at the ways you enjoy expressing them. What do you love to do? What makes you happy? What is it you dream of becoming? These are the questions that lead you to your purpose. (p. 181)

If this is the case, then one of our primary goals is to help our students find out what they are good at, what they love, and what they will be happy doing for a lifetime. This entails developing lessons and strategies that will provide the widest possible range of opportunities for students to try out various avenues of expression. Help them to develop into creative problem solvers as well as critical thinkers. Honor their questions and their need for a safe, fun-filled environment so that they will take risks and stretch themselves beyond what they or you could imagine. These are the elements that spark engagement at the deepest levels.

We can't afford to ever miss a chance to verbalize what talent, gift, or skill we see in the students we teach. If we notice a child with a great deal of emotional intelligence, we must tell him so and talk about jobs that he would find satisfying as well as what college major would best complement that strength. If we have a good writer, we must talk about careers in which she could use this talent. We must mold assignments that give the artist a chance to show off his abilities, the musician a way to put her talents to good use in class, and the leader the reins to lead. This is the best use of our own talent, our own purpose as a teacher.

Sir Kenneth Robinson's book *The Element* (2009) includes narratives about how and when people discovered their creative talents and what journeys they took to see their passions unfold. Many of these stories revealed how small a role their school experiences played in their self-actualization. Sadly, many spoke of their school experiences as even playing a detrimental role in this regard. We need to change that.

Having studied student engagement in high school classrooms from the perspective of the flow theory for which he has become world famous, Mihaly Csikszentmihalyi concludes:

> The results of the present study suggest that activities that are academically intense and foster positive emotions stand the best chance of engaging students. Ideally, teachers may develop activities that are experienced as challenging and relevant, yet also allow students to feel in control of their learning environment and confident in their ability. These are activities in which students concentrate, experience enjoyment, and are provided with immediate, intrinsic satisfaction that builds a foundation of interest for the future. Teachers succeeding in providing such engagement most likely consider not only the knowledge and skills to be learned, but also the students as learners, adapting instruction to their developmental levels and individual interests. (Shernoff, Csikszentmihalyi, Schneider, & Shernoff, 2003, p. 172)

Meaning for children is found in challenging environments where choice and a feeling of control are prevalent; where an atmosphere of confidence, positive emotions, and satisfaction exists; and where stress is limited. When these elements are present, student engagement is assured. Infusing our lessons with meaning and relevance ensures more than engagement, however; it ensures that our children will have a grasp of self and realize there are multiple doors open to worlds of possibility. Learning to wield the tool of meaning carefully and intentionally is an important part of a teacher's life's work.

Multiple Intelligences and Project-Based Learning

If the pursuit of meaning is a tool of engagement, then its working parts are project-based learning and a knowledge and consequent use of multiple intelligences. Learning should not only prepare one for life, but also provide a meaningful experience in the present. Students enjoy learning when learning makes sense and simply do not pay attention to what is boring.

Working on real problems is a major thrust of project-based learning. Projects assist students in succeeding within the classroom and beyond by allowing them to apply multiple intelligences in completing a project that yields intrinsic satisfaction. A call for 21st century skills is a call for opportunities to develop individuals who can solve problems creatively, using the wide array of multiple strengths they possess.

Teachers need more practice and leeway in forming learning frameworks that allow their students to choose their own approaches to open-ended projects that take advantage of their individual interests and strengths. Teachers are still using traditional teaching strategies that tend to focus on verbal/linguistic and mathematical/logical intelligences alone even though research recommends the exercise of strategies that address multiple intelligences and less traditional learning modalities.

The research on project-based learning tends to agree that it is more effective than traditional rote, teacher-centered methods, but, as educational consultant Jane L. David (2008) concludes, because of the complexity of project-based learning, the environment must provide skilled instructors who have access to well-designed projects and are provided with support from the administration. If this isn't available, the efforts at project-based learning can easily sink to providing unrelated lessons with no clear focus. However, David does state that "teachers can use the key ideas underlying project-based learning in some measure in any classroom. Using real-life problems to motivate students, challenging them to think deeply about meaningful content, and enabling them to work collaboratively are practices that yield benefits for all students" (p. 82).

Feedback Using Formative Assessment

Providing feedback is one of the teacher's primary duties. The quality and timeliness of that feedback are key in determining the level of student learning and engagement and the effectiveness of student-teacher relationships.

Timely, specific feedback is the foremost motivator for the brain. John Hattie, director of Visible Learning Laboratories, analyzed nearly eight thousand studies on teaching effectiveness and concluded that the most powerful single modification that a teacher could make to his or her current pedagogy that would enhance achievement is feedback. The way in which feedback is offered to a child influences that child's future ability to attack new learning with confidence or withdraw into hopelessness (Hattie, 1992).

We are all cognizant of the current emphasis on the necessity for summative feedback—standardized testing, high-stakes assessments, end-of-course graded exams. These seldom serve as good sources of meaningful feedback because of the time lag between administering these tests and receiving the results.

Formative assessment feedback, on the other hand, is a powerful and potentially constructive tool for learning and engagement because of the immediacy of its timing and the informality of its setting. The essence of formative assessment is its process of feedback, which occurs during instruction using a broad range of activities from performance tasks to short but thorough conversations between the student and teacher over the work at hand. Paul Black and Dylan Wiliam, experts in the field of classroom assessment and educational standards, explain that true formative assessment occurs when the evidence of how a student is performing is actually used by the teacher to adapt his or her teaching or used by the student to adapt his or her skill performance. More precisely, quality formative assessments are meaningful when students' thinking processes are examined so that changes can be made by both the teacher and the students to better reach mastery of understanding and performance. The outcome of the feedback offered by good formative assessments is student engagement because as students become aware of what and how they are learning, they become more motivated and consequently more engaged (Black & Wiliam, 1998a).

Researchers Robert Marzano, Debra Pickering, and Jane Pollock (2001) synthesized Hattie's research on feedback to provide the following guidelines for the classroom:

1. Feedback should be "corrective" in nature. This means that it should provide students with an explanation of what they are doing that is correct and what they are doing that is not correct.

2. Feedback should be timely. Feedback provided immediately after assessment enhances learning.

3. Feedback should be specific to a criterion; that is, it should inform students where they stand relative to a specific target of knowledge or skill. Research has consistently indicated that criterion-referenced feedback has a more powerful effect on student learning than norm-referenced feedback.

4. Students can effectively provide some of their own feedback by monitoring their own progress. (as quoted in McTighe & Seif, 2004, p. 12)

In an extensive study on formative assessment—including the review of 580 reports or chapters in more than 160 journals—Black and Wiliam concluded that they know of no other single method verified to raise standards and no better way of raising achievement than strong formative assessment of daily classroom work (Black & Wiliam, 1998a). They also found that with improved formative assessment, low achievers raised their performance even more than other students. These gains are especially important since these are the pupils who often come to see themselves as unable to learn, become disengaged, and usually cease to take school seriously. These are the students who cause disruptions in the classroom, have low attendance, are labeled as the "at risk" population, and tend to drop out.

Feedback from authentic formative assessment is certainly a golden instrument in the toolbox of the teacher trying to reach the hard-to-reach students and lift the engagement quotient of the entire class. There is a need for caution, though. Formative assessment is not simply giving out short quizzes periodically during the class period for the purpose of determining if students are mastering discrete pieces of information. Teachers are very conscientious about collecting data like this—marking work and placing results in gradebooks—but they are not as thorough when giving students individual feedback on how to improve and what strategies to use to master the skills that are needed. True feedback of this kind is collaborative and ongoing throughout the day. Though textbook publishers and test creators are aggressively campaigning for a market in creating formative assessments in the format of mini-tests inserted at specific points in the curriculum, authentic formative assessments are far from generic, one-size-fits-all items pulled from a test bank.

In a letter to blogger Anthony Cody, who is a National Board–certified teacher and an active member of the Teacher Leaders Network, J. Myron Atkin writes,

They [Black and Wiliam] also have been very clear about exactly what formative assessment is: working with a student, or a group of students, to develop a course of action that helps bridge the gap between current student knowledge and the desired educational goal. Providing feedback that is usable, detailed, and often individualized is at the heart of this kind of assessment. (Cody, 2009)

Asking for exit slips to determine understanding, utilizing peer reviews, scheduling one-on-one conferences on writing progress—all are examples of actively gathering formative feedback during the teaching process. In contrast, some districts are buying programs that require teachers to bubble in the progress regarding one hundred items students must master per grading period per student as their answer to improving formative assessment. That isn't it.

Technology: A Dynamic, Ever-Changing Tool

It is simply common sense in this era of digital natives to acknowledge that technology is one of the most powerful engagement tools in teachers' toolboxes. To ignore the influence of technology on today's children is to make ourselves completely irrelevant and incomprehensible to our students. Researchers Mizuko Ito and associates spent three years conducting over five thousand hours of online observations as well as over eight hundred interviews in what is called the most extensive study of media use by adolescents thus far. Not surprisingly, they determined social networking, video-sharing abilities, online games, and ownership of technological equipment such as iPods and cell phones to be common fixtures in the lives and cultures of most youth today. A small percentage use these media to explore interests and find information; the majority of use is "friendship driven" (Ito et al., 2008).

Teachers are well aware of this—they are constantly asking students to put away their cell phones and their iPod earphones, and pay attention. Many look at these gadgets as disruptions, annoyances, irritating and troublesome interferences getting in the way of their efforts at instruction. Some teachers, however, are trying to tame these technological appliances and embed their use, their appeal, and their engaging qualities into instruction.

Cell phones are maturing quickly into handheld Web browsers that can have a dynamic influence on classrooms as research and learning tools. Practically all cell phones have picture-taking and audio capabilities and could be used in class investigative assignments, interviews, or visualization opportunities. The new world of technological advancements has only begun. Harnessing the technology will help teachers harness their students as well.

Another type of technology that is entering the educational world is online learning accessibility. Some districts are sticking their toes into this deep pool of possibilities to be able to assist students with courses that are not possible for their budgets or staff to offer. Some districts are currently experimenting with webinars as a source of both professional development and classroom instruction. The U.S. Department of Education, Office of Planning, Evaluation, and Policy Development, Policy and Program Studies Service (2009) conducted

> a systematic search of the research literature from 1996 through July 2008 and identified more than a thousand empirical studies of online learning. Analysts screened these studies to find those that (a) contrasted an online to a face-to-face condition, (b) measured student learning outcomes, (c) used a rigorous research design, and (d) provided adequate information to calculate an effect size. As a result of this screening, 51 independent effects were identified that could be subjected to meta-analysis. *The meta-analysis found that, on average, students in online learning conditions performed better than those receiving face-to-face instruction.* (p. ix)

This research is primarily focused on higher education but is likely to eventually have ramifications on high school instruction. As the study shows, online learning is more engaging and more productive than face-to-face situations. Quiet, usually uninvolved students have access to the instructor immediately through chat-board systems, providing them with the contact they don't experience in the classroom. Feedback on assignments is usually more extensive and timely. Students feel a sense of control over the learning and the pace of learning, control that isn't available in the average classroom setting. All these factors can help us reinvent ourselves in the classroom and become more sensitive to individual needs, allowing us to customize our instruction to fit those needs.

The subject of technology in education is too broad and well documented to be covered in this small section of focus. Educators are aware that technology has a vital role to play in enabling data-driven decision making and are becoming more and more computer savvy as instructors. Classrooms are being outfitted with interactive whiteboards connected to teachers' computers, clickers, and more. The point is that technology is a tool for better instruction in all its shapes, sizes, and forms. Technology is a potent vehicle for immediate feedback, the brain's foremost motivator. It is not going away. Students are caught up in its relevance to their lives outside of the classroom, and tapping into its appeal will only heighten our ability to connect with them and engage them in learning within our classrooms.

Steps Toward Solutions

Engagement is more than students simply sitting quietly, paying attention to their teachers and to one another. At its

*best, engagement is activation of students' heads, hearts,
and spirit, and a recognition that students are full partners
in the teaching/learning process, not merely its recipients.
From my reading of the literature in this area and my experience, one of the most powerful methods for promoting
student engagement is context-rich, project-based learning
with peers, particularly when projects are focused on the
solution of problems that are meaningful to students.*

—Dennis Sparks

There are several different tools available to choose from when creating your own engagement toolbox. Don't be overwhelmed; use your imagination and have fun. This section offers exercises to get you started.

Put a Camera to Good Use

The camera is quite effective at attracting student interest and participation. Following are just a few of the many ways you can use your camera to access your students' goodwill and involvement:

- If you have a system for designating the student of the week, make that student's picture the background wallpaper for your computer during the week as well.

- When you make up your seating chart at the beginning of the year, take three or four group pictures, cut out the heads, and tape them to the names on the seating chart. If you teach multiple classes, this serves as a great cheat sheet for those first few days and later helps a substitute teacher keep names and faces straight. Students love to check the seating charts and demand that they be changed at the semester because they are so much more "grown up."

- Don't forget to take your camera to extracurricular events. Taking pictures of your students and posting them in the classroom sends a clear message that you are aware of their outside interests and care about them.

- Add students' pictures to their final drafts, and display these outside your door. Knowing that their pictures might be added to their papers might be just the push some need to see that the work is of better quality than usual.

- Take a class portrait at the end of the year to add to the other classes you have taught over the years. This is a great tradition maker.

- If you are using PowerPoint presentations to teach specific skills or materials, insert pictures of your own students when possible. This keeps attention riveted to your screen.

- Embed short videos of students learning into your PowerPoint presentations to reinforce material for reviews. Be sure to have gathered permissions from parents to film or photograph students for educational use beforehand. Look into your school's policy on such permission slips.

- Allow students the use of cameras to research various topics in their local vicinities. (These might be low-cost disposable cameras that go on sale when their expiration date comes due, or you can sometimes get donated cameras from PTA groups, local organizations, and so forth.) Tap in to the picture-taking capability of students' cell phones. Instead of treating them as problems, use them as learning instruments.

- Bring in pictures of yourself at the same age of your students.

- Use picture activities as good old bribes: "While reading this book, make a list of scenes that would be good to photograph to make a storyboard. We will then dress up and pretend we are the characters and represent key scenes in the book. Of course, you have to read the book before we can do this."

Go Online

Providing meaningful educational opportunities is the goal of many organizations that post contests, lesson plans, and support help for teachers online. Start a page in the back of your lesson plan book on which to copy good websites that you discover or are recommended by others. Set a goal of investigating a new website at least once a month. Following is just a sampling of such offerings (visit **go.solution-tree.com/instruction** for live links to the websites in this book):

- The Wonder Rotunda (www.wonderrotunda.com) allows adults to create their own avatar and join a child on a visit through the site. The Wonder Rotunda blends game play with rich educational content. With an emphasis on stimulating curiosity and learning, it is an alternative to the Internet's typical offerings for kids. Wonder Rotunda is not a social network and does not contain ads.

- Teaching Songs and Chants Developed by Teachers for Teachers (www.teachersworkshop.com/twshop/songschants.html), compiled by William Bender, is a website geared toward elementary students and has songs and chants for all subjects.

- A New Home for the Shebs (www.montgomeryschoolsmd.org /schools/cabinjohnms/lessons/science/dss_web/shebs/shebs.htm) is a project-based unit on the solar system for seventh-grade students. Shebs have lost their home and found themselves in our solar system. They need to find a new place to colonize. Their unique characteristics make it difficult to identify their most suitable environment. The survival of their race is dependent on their ability to find a new home quickly. Can you find them the best home in our solar system before time runs out?

- The Buck Institute for Education (www.bie.org/index.php/site/PBL /resources/Project_Examples) provides a variety of examples of project-based learning.

- Math Resources from PBS (www.pbs.org/teachers/_files/pdf/PBS _Math_resources.pdf) offers links to several project-based learning opportunities. Visit www.pbs.org/teachers for many more on-air and online math resources.

- Designed for K–12 student teams of all interest, skill, and ability levels, ExploraVision (www.exploravision.org) encourages kids to create and explore a vision of future technology by combining their imaginations with the tools of science.

- PBS Teachers Science & Tech (www.pbs.org/teachers/sciencetech) provides links to science and technology content that has been contextualized within grade-subject pages.

- ReadWriteThink (www.readwritethink.org/lessons) provides a lesson plan index. You can sort the lessons by title, grade, or date by clicking on the appropriate header.

- The JASON Project (www.jason.org) is a multimedia, interdisciplinary science program for grades 4–9.

- A to Z Teacher Stuff (http://atozteacherstuff.com) is a teacher-created site designed to help teachers find online resources for successful lessons. It offers applications for word-search generators, a database of leveled books, printable handouts, and discussion sites.

Examine Your Formative Feedback

How often have we complained about results from our students' high-stakes tests taking too long to arrive to help improve instruction? By the time we get them, we have a new set of students with different needs and strengths. To be of value, feedback needs to be timely and specific. Following is a set of questions regarding feedback, especially formative feedback. Answer as many as you can:

- How would you explain to another teacher your system for using formative assessment feedback with your students?

- Make a list of your informal and formal interactions with students for the purpose of providing feedback on their work and offering advice and suggestions on how to improve their performance.

- How many students do you usually interact with in order to provide feedback during a class period?

- Do you work with your students while they are doing seatwork, or do you wait to mark papers as a group when everyone is finished?

- What is more important: accumulating scores on assignments or seeing to it that students recognize what can be improved and how to go about making those improvements? How do you exhibit this to your students?

Examine Your and Your Students' Knowledge of Technology

We find it difficult to even think about living without today's technology. Our children are considered digital natives, and we who are older and can remember when there were rotary dials and only a few channels on the television are labeled digital immigrants. We are wise to take advantage of the savvy our students possess and the ease with which they can acclimate themselves to technology. Investigate your relationship to technology as a learning and engagement tool. The following will help you get started:

1. Find out just what your students are able to do with technology when they are not in your classroom. Administer a survey of the technology your students have at their disposal. Have them walk through their houses and jot down everything that could be called "technology." Use the results as the basis for a class discussion.

2. Have students help you make a list of their current technological skills. Can they burn information to a DVD? Can they work an iPhone or an iPad or a digital video camera? While making this list, make an auxiliary list of technological vocabulary. An activity students find fascinating is discussing the metaphors we use when we talk about computers and computer functions, such as throwing files into the trash, cutting and pasting, using file folders, and so on.

3. Insert possible options into your lessons and assignments that could utilize the students' technological skills.

4. Organize a session with other teachers for sharing and teaching new technology and discuss how it can be used in lessons.

Reflection on the Engagement Toolbox

Look at this chapter as you would look at a home improvement store. Instead of being overwhelmed by the number of tools available for every possible job, choose a couple that are easy to use and seem to fit your specific needs now, and then choose a couple that you would like to focus on in more depth. Write them down and discuss why you chose them and how you intend to implement them.

_____

_____

_____

_____

_____

_____

_____

_____

_____

_____

_____

_____

_____

One new strategy you might try out this week:

_____

Creativity

We need to provide our students with opportunities to use and understand their abilities to think divergently, creatively, analytically, and critically if we are going to educate the whole child for the 21st century. The current emphasis on high-stakes testing requires a great deal of creativity to find ways to limit stress and deeply engage students in more rigorous material. This chapter provides a look at the nature of creativity and how students feel about it; it also illustrates how creative approaches to instruction spark curiosity, interest, and ultimately engagement.

First Thoughts on Creativity

Think about your personal experiences with creativity—when did you first recognize it, who strengthened it, how did your schooling nurture it? Then think about what role you feel creativity plays in your teaching, especially in how you engage your students.

Notes From the Field

The five following pieces are from two high school writing classes I visited. I asked the students to comment on their experiences with creativity in and out of school. These are samples of the responses.

Katelyn writes:

> Creativity has always been a part of my life, for as long as I can remember. The seed was sown as a child when my mother began encouraging me to dive deeply into every book I could get my hands on. From there, my mind went wild. I wanted to create my own characters, write my own stories. And today, creativity has taken my life hostage. When it flares up, it starts as a small brushing against the inside of my mind, a creative idea lazily trying to escape. But if I ignore it, the creative idea becomes frantic, and it screams and pounds against my skull until I hand it a pencil and let it dig its way out. But as well as being my captor, creativity has been my friend, too. After a long day, a hard breakup, or whatever else it might be, my creativity takes me gently by the hand and leads me to a land of my own creation where I control the people, control all the emotions, control the outcomes of everything I am helpless to control in the real world. Creativity has shaped who I am, helps me to see the buried beauty in everything. . . .

Kyle writes:

> To be creative, the teacher has to be on the same level as the students. They have to sometimes come to the level of the students, and sometimes expect the students to come up to the maturity level of the teacher. Even if it's a little joke to loosen the mood, making the students comfortable enough to learn, this is huge in my mind. I am always 100% more likely to do extra work or go the creative extra mile for teachers who care and I can relate to.

Abbie says:

> In seventh grade, my crazy, funny, innovative teacher gave me the confidence to bring out my creativity with her loud and strange lessons and projects. That and my mom's uniqueness have helped me become who I am today.

Jeffrey writes:

> When I was in fifth grade, we were doing math problems. I came up with a creative, efficient way to speed up the solving of these math problems, but I freaked out my teacher and was accused for doing so. I didn't try that again.

Bo writes:

> There is not much creativity at all in school now. We don't do many fun activities or group activities which make things exciting. I am normally bored out of my mind every day. Today the activity you had us all do with the baggies filled with little items as metaphors was a good activity. It made me want to pay attention. You are a good teacher who gives us the excitement we all need. Thanks.

The Discussion

Bo's opinion is one that is often heard in the upper grades. It brings to mind a question posed by Patricia Vakos (2010), a teacher at Ocean Lakes High School in Virginia, in her essay "Why the Blank Stare? Strategies for Visual Learners":

> Why do we creatively present materials using manipulatives and visuals almost exclusively in elementary school classes, yet subject students to almost exclusive oral learning techniques in high-school classes? What happened to the excitement and thought-processing? Are the learners in elementary school really that different from those in a high-school setting? In the current climate of high-stakes testing and mandated curriculum, creative and innovative teaching is perhaps more important than ever as it keeps classrooms energetic places of learning.

Bo would agree. As students age, we seem to educate them less and less as whole human beings with bodies and emotions. We focus more and more on their brains—and on the left side of their brains at that. As Sir Kenneth Robinson often says, we tend to systematically strip-mine our children's brains for only one type of intelligence—critical, analytical thinking—and completely ignore, or worse, belittle, the other intelligences.

Creative methods of engagement that tap into more than a single intelligence are apt to be effective in the upper grades simply because they are so rarely integrated into instruction. Bo described the classroom visit as "exciting," and it "made [him] want to pay attention." He writes that he is "normally bored out of [his] mind every day." The brain is simply not interested in the common, everyday stuff; this is boring.

So, just what was so exciting about my visit? Not that much. The golden rule of engagement is that anything that isn't on an 8½ × 11 page in black and white is by its very nature interesting! Even something as simple as cutting whole pages in half for students to write on is likely to get better participation responses than leaving those sheets whole. The corollaries to that golden rule are: anything by way of writing materials that veers away from the usual, that isn't the status quo, especially if it's in color, is always far more interesting. Following that, anything one can touch or hold trumps the written word. With that in mind, I created baggies that held objects that served as metaphors illustrating the nature of creativity. Inside were:

- **An eraser**. To be more creative, both teachers and students must lose their fear of being wrong. These little round erasers had smiley faces on them to show that making mistakes isn't nearly as bad a situation as we are subtly led to believe. Teachers need to nurture risk taking in their classes, not cultivate in the students a fear of making mistakes or not giving the right answers.

- **A wiggly eyeball**. Author Anais Nin said, "We don't see things as they are, we see them as we are." Creative people stop their mind's chatter for a while and look around with fresh eyes. When we slow down and really look at people, the world, and ourselves, we can't help but be overwhelmed by the beauty. Imagination begins with our *eyes*.

- **A tiny wrapped present**. This symbolized living in the "present"— not in the past or in the future but in the reality of the now. It was also a reminder that surprise is the hallmark of creativity. We should train ourselves to make it a point to surprise someone daily and build our own sensitivity to the surprises that we encounter. Surprise energizes us and enables us to look at life freshly and with anticipation. A good way to increase one's creativity is to make surprise an *everyday* habit.

- **A bottle of bubbles**. Most students found this tiny bottle to be the most novel. Everyone wanted to try them out. The bubbles grew, released from the wands, floated before us, then popped and disappeared. And so do our ideas. The most dreaded tragedy for a creative person is to lose those great ideas that suddenly appear in the mind—to allow them to disappear before they can be written down. My admonition to the students was to respect their personal bubbles of creative thought; don't let them pop and disappear forever.

- **An artificial diamond**. These diamonds were used to represent the quality of the students' work. A kind of mantra I learned from Julia Cameron, author of *The Artist's Way*, is that our job is to produce *quantity* and the universe will decide the *quality*. I stress this when I talk to students about their writing: just keep doing it, and you'll find that those diamonds will begin to shine through.

- **A card on how to nurture creativity** (from a deck of *52 Ways to Nurture Your Creativity* by Lynn Gordon). One of the more interesting qualities of creativity is how it is stimulated by randomness. Each student received a random card and was asked to think about how that statement referred to him or her. The intention was to encourage a stream of thought in the student that offered an insight into his or her creative abilities.

- **A star stickpin**. The star represents the need to celebrate successes, to acknowledge accomplishments. One of the staunchest blocks to utilizing one's creativity is fear—a fear of failing, but also a fear of succeeding. Both are capable of crippling us. Success causes us to stand out. It might require us to move away emotionally from the group we are associated with. It changes our status with our friends and family. It may even cause us to change our view of ourselves. It takes as much courage to accept our success as it does to accept our failures. That's why there's a stickpin behind the star—to remind us that we should accept our success and not run from it.

- **A small Slinky and a ruler**. These two items are perfect metaphors for describing the difference between creative and critical thinking processes. The ruler, straight and static, represents the step-by-step method of critical thinking. The Slinky represents the essence of creative thinking. It stretches, bounces, and loops back on itself, and it is only concerned with the end result, not the method of getting there.

- **A paperclip in the form of a foot**. This little foot was the item most prized by my young audience. It symbolized an admonition to the students: keep on the path, never give up on your talent, do not forget your gifts in the pursuit of transitory wealth or security, be bold, and follow your dreams and inner yearnings. Just put one foot before the other, and the journey will take you where you are meant to go.

Katelyn came to grips with her creative bubbles by allowing them to have free rein. Jeffrey, on the other hand, had the experience of being stuck by the star stickpin. His successful idea was rejected by his teacher, and he never forgot the experience. Kyle's and Abbie's teachers provided an atmosphere in which they felt safe enough to be themselves, to try out their fledgling creative wings and not worry when they needed to use the eraser. Kyle's, Abbie's, and Bo's remarks also made the connection between creativity and engagement.

What Is Creativity?

What is creativity? Here is a brief look:

- It's an outside-of-the-box experience—lateral rather than vertical thinking.

- It's a way to get students to do what we want them to do because rigor without motivation won't fly!

- It's not about fluff or fancy bulletin boards, but about effective teaching strategies.

- It's finding an alternate entry point for frontloading activities.

- It's using cross-fertilization of various subject matters to break down compartmentalized thinking, to see the bigger picture.

- It's embedding opportunities to confront randomness and seek out patterns. To children, puzzle pieces seem random at first, but as they look more closely, they see the patterns develop.

- It's employing and augmenting risk taking rather than insulating students from it.

- It's what is necessary to devise differentiated lessons and to implement RTI successfully.

- It's rethinking what we see, embracing a tolerance of differences, and not being crippled by the fear of making mistakes.

- It's working with real-life scenarios and exercising both of the brain's hemispheres.

- It's being the most authentic teacher—alive and in touch with the art of teaching.

When teachers allow students to explore their own methods of expression, there is a built-in guarantee of engagement. Creativity necessitates freedom of choice, personalization, a sense of play, internal rewards, and challenges that configure to meet the skill and interest levels of the child. It takes a courageous teacher to set up the circumstances that allow students to work with such parameters. Yet these are the conditions that allow for differentiation, mastery learning, whole child awareness, multi-intelligence instruction, response to intervention, and a deeper investigation of subject matter through the utilization of higher-order thinking. These are the conditions for high achievement.

Necessary Conditions for Creative Learning and Teaching

The students' quotes reveal that creative expression isn't the norm in formal education but rather a rare and prized commodity. Students must be led by intrinsic motivation to participate in reflective creative learning, whereas extrinsic rewards are more serviceable when concentrating on the memorization of low-level skills and noncreative information. Caine and Caine (1994) cite numerous studies that explain why our current system of rewards and punishments in the form of everything from smiley faces to grades inhibits intrinsic motivation and diminishes creativity. Sadly, a system of rewards and punishments can be "selectively de-motivating in the long term, particularly when others have control over the system. It reduces the desire as well as the capacity of learners to engage in original thought" (Caine & Caine, 1994, p. 77). Harvard professor Teresa Amabile (1985) affirms that the more complex the activity, the more it's hurt by extrinsic rewards. She also makes the point that extrinsic rewards are most destructive when offered to individuals attempting creative tasks and challenges that require higher-order thinking and problem solving.

Our school systems are not structured to provide students with the necessary elements for higher-level creative thought—an abundance of unstructured time, a high degree of choice, an opportunity for ideas to incubate, stress-free play without competition and ranking, and an opportunity to shift gears and drop projects that have lost their appeal—but teachers can supply and nurture an environment for creative thinking that becomes the rule and not the exception. What does that environment contain? According to Edward Deci and Richard Ryan (1985), two of the most respected early voices in research on motivation, creativity is facilitated by autonomy and choice, a decrease in stress and pressure, the presence of a positive emotional tone, trust, and higher self-esteem, among other elements. Psychologist Jerome Bruner (1965) argues that children should be encouraged to "treat a task as a problem for which one invents an answer, rather than finding one out there in a book or on the blackboard" (pp. 1013–1014).

And what of our own creativity? We too need the same conditions to maximize our resources. Our success is directly related to our ability to utilize our personal creativity. Caine and Caine (2001) confirm this:

> One of the hallmarks of great teachers is that they can vary a general approach in order to accommodate the enormous differences that exist from child to child. However, it is only in flexible environments that such high level teaching can be effective. (p. 24)

The ability "to accommodate the enormous differences that exist from child to child" is no longer looked upon as something we find solely in the classrooms of great teachers. It is now viewed as a necessary skill for all teachers to possess and is described under the labels of "differentiation" and "RTI," to name a couple. The element that allows and produces such seamless variation in approach is teacher creativity.

Misconceptions About Creativity

To many, the notion that creativity can be serious seems to be a contradiction. The common perception of creativity is that it is fun and simplistic, lacking depth of cognitive effort or value. This is the kind of thinking that has warped the development of a systematic study of creative thought processes, causing tremendous damage. Many feel that creativity is simply an exercise in brainstorming and the freedom to suggest any idea no matter how outrageous (de Bono, 1992). This misconception exists not only in the professional worlds of research, business, economics, and medicine but, most importantly, in the world of education at all levels.

Administrators hate fluff, and with good reason. The teacher who conducts fun activities that have no relationship to the curriculum goals or standards is the teacher who destroys the safe environment for true creative teaching for everyone. Every strategy and activity of good, effective teaching is thoroughly embedded in the unit or lesson for a specific purpose. The effective innovative, creative teacher knows *why* a project or strategy is valuable, can explain and defend its worth, and can show how it reinforces the central purpose of the lesson.

Most negative attitudes concerning creativity likely flow from a prior knowledge of someone who has misused and misdirected creativity. Other negative attitudes may stem from a sense of uneasiness at how messy creative activities can appear to be—how a classroom may seem to be on the verge of chaos from an outsider's point of view. And the truth is that some classrooms are and some aren't on that verge of chaos at times. However, "brain-based learning theories uphold that classrooms that are noisy, active environments where students are engaged in individual learning paths can be conducive to students learning at high levels" (Wilson, 2004). Yet to many, it seems so much more efficient to *tell* students something than to allow them to discover and work it out for themselves. A quiet room seems so much more disciplined than a noisy one. Disciplined, yes, but not always educationally alive.

We need to strip the connotations of fluff and form a picture of creativity as a serious thinking tool that facilitates problem discovering and problem solving. Pann Baltz, involved in the Creative Classroom Project, writes:

> Although most people might look for signs of creativity in the appearance of the bulletin boards, student made projects, centers and displays in the classroom, I feel the truly creative classroom goes way beyond what can be seen with the eyes. It is a place where bodies and minds actively pursue new knowledge. Having a creative classroom means that the teacher takes risks on a daily basis and encourages his/her students to do the same. (as quoted in Morris, 2006)

Creativity is found in Abbie's seventh-grade classroom with her teacher's loud and strange lessons and projects. Creativity is found in Kyle's experience of being expected to come up to the maturity level of the teacher. Creativity is found in Katelyn's abundance of intrinsic motivation ready to be tapped by any teacher willing and able. Seeking and recognizing true creativity and what copious rewards it can bring to your classroom are important milestones along the path to engagement.

Novelty Within Ritual

As humans, we are a paradox of needs. We need uniformity; we need variety. We need ritual; we need novelty. Our brains delight equally in order and chaos; both are necessary to satisfy us (Jensen, 2003; Sousa, 1998).

Our students' brains want two seemingly opposed learning situations. They want the safety, comfort, and assurance of predictability that ritual offers, and at the same time, they want the curiosity, piqued interest, and focus that novelty provides. If novelty is missing from the instructional day, a deadening boredom sets in. If there is too much novelty and no consistency, confusion clouds the child's ability to focus and learn. As with all strategies and instructional methods, balance is the final judge of efficacy.

This basic concept is important to ensuring student engagement in the classroom yet is often not understood by developers of instructional programs—especially those who have not spent much time in the classroom. The underlying flaw in many of these systems of instruction is that they are strong on ritual but lacking in novelty. They become so unbearably boring to both the teacher and the students that in order to survive in a classroom, the teacher needs to put down the system and find something to wake and engage the class. However, the pressure on teachers to provide "fidelity of implementation" (Fixsen, Naoom, Blase, Friedman, & Wallace, 2005), referring to the delivery of instruction in the way in which it was designed to be delivered—in other words, to keep going with the program no matter what—is so intense in some areas that there is little room left to pull out anything that isn't tied to the system, anything that could possibly ignite and engage the class. Engaging students when so little room is allowed for change is not easy. Carefully read what the program demands and what is considered open for the teacher's good judgment and discretion. Find the loopholes.

What appears logically and analytically reasonable in a program that is based on consistency of application and data gathering just doesn't take into consideration the human need for change. Teachers who face children day in and day out know this in their very bones. Dragging our charges kicking and yelling—or worse, silent and numb—through a curriculum program and testing schedule devoid of excitement, challenge, meaningful complex tasks, choice, and enjoyment is not going to provide us with long-term achievement. It might boost scores temporarily, but it will do little to stimulate innovative problem solving and deep understanding.

The essence of novelty is that it is a new, seldom repeated activity. Novelty isn't an add-on but rather a very real need in response to today's environment, which is wiring children's brains differently than in the past. Children are developing in an environment rich in rapid sensory and emotional changes from a multimedia-based culture. They are accustomed to responding to activities and stimuli of short duration. If you doubt this, please turn on MTV for a few minutes, and notice the flow of changing images that play heavily on the viewer's emotions. The brains of today's students are far more responsive to the unique or different—the novel—than those of years ago, and yet the schools haven't changed. Students are finding the slower pace of the school's delivery of information—in contrast to the world they know outside of the school day—to be boring and unengaging. They see little novelty, considerably more predictability, and little relevance. Consequently, their attention spans are shorter, they have more difficulty focusing, and they are more easily distracted. These children are not "educationally defective"; they are just different from those who haven't grown up in today's environment (Sousa, 1998).

A novel activity is fun the first time, OK the second, and boring the third. This is why the creative teacher is always on the lookout for fresh material and strategies. Teachers can be taught to hunt novel strategies with the same efficacy that they can learn to perform any teaching skill. Adding novelty to a teacher's delivery of instruction is a topic that has been woefully neglected and could be helped by a stronger emphasis in teacher training. Novelty is just as important as ritual to good, effective planning for optimal instruction.

Creative teachers break routines to get students' attention and turn predictable procedures into not-so-predictable procedures. For example, instead of giving every student a book, give each a chapter of a book. (Tear the chapters out of the original book, staple the pages together, and put each chapter into a labeled five-by-eight envelope.) Students silently read their chapters, then begin the process of storytelling. Provide a scaffolding guide sheet for collecting information that matches up with the two or three chosen areas of focus. The class intently listens to a student narrate his or her chapter, asks questions to clarify information, takes notes, then moves to the next student. Each student's reading assignment is important to the group as it is necessary for everyone's understanding of the book. This exercise hits listening skills, summarizing abilities, comprehension, note taking, questioning—all in a "novel" context.

Creative teachers also utilize another element of novelty that has nothing to do with props or activities: word choice. After years in the educational system, students develop a cognitive and emotional aversion to certain terms and phrases that are everyday staples of the educational vocabulary. Just mention the word *grammar* to high school students, and you'll see the lights go out and a glaze form over their eyes. However, we can sneak in the back door of the student brain by rewording overused educational terms. The word *test* can trigger negativity and stymie the student's ability to perform. Why not call it a chance to show off what you know? Or a snapshot of the brain in action? The emotional weight of words has an impressive effect on a child's desire and ability to engage. Replace those worn-out words, and breathe fresh air into those rituals of education. This is using creative novelty.

Steps Toward Solutions

The key question isn't "What fosters creativity?" But it is why in God's name isn't everyone creative? Where was the human potential lost? How was it crippled? I think therefore a good question might be not why do people create? But why do people not create or innovate? We have got to abandon that sense of amazement in the face of creativity, as if it were a miracle if anybody created anything.

—Abraham Maslow

Many of us have been conditioned to shy away from anything that smacks of the "creative" for fear that we will be looked upon as demanding less rigorous learning or wasting time with unnecessary fluff. Viewing creative or divergent thinking as just as legitimate an operation of our brains' processes as analytical or critical thinking is the hallmark of the teacher who educates the whole child. The following exercises are meant to help both you and your students develop a more positive affinity toward and awareness of creative ability.

Gather Creative Experiences

Ask your students to write about their ideas of and experiences with creativity. This assignment can then be used as the basis for a whole-class discussion. You can chart what students believe creativity is, how it can be incorporated in their class work, and how it should be judged. Such an activity gives your class the understanding that you do indeed value creative efforts and intend to acknowledge them.

Don't Do All the Work Yourself

Beware of overplanning! One pitfall in the quest to set up a creative project or assignment is making the directions so specific that you end up with a paint-by-numbers kind of activity—all the opportunities for actual creative thought have been taken by the teacher! This can be avoided by paying careful attention to the rubric you make. Point out where the student choices are located and what conformities to format and written conventions are required.

Examine the directions you typically give students when asking them to produce creative projects. Mark the places where you give them the opportunity to make choices. How robust and meaningful are the choices? When developing your next set of directions for such an activity, try to let go of micromanaging and urge the students to become choosers as well as doers.

Check Your Use of Novelty

Go over your monthly lesson plans, and see what your ratio of novelty to ritual has been. How long did it take before your teaching routines rolled into ruts that slowed down your engagement wheels and bogged down you and your class in boredom? Mark places where you could have inserted more novelty into your teaching and perhaps avoided breaking your momentum.

When writing your new plans, make room for a place in your lesson plan book to signal use of novelty in your delivery. For instance, you might begin class with an oral check-in activity such as having students answer a question like "What is your favorite electronic gadget?" to establish their presence. Such an activity takes very little time but provides great novelty.

Move for Change

So what does novelty look like in the day-to-day classroom? Novelty is the offspring of any type of change. Consider a change in location:

- Move around the room so that students never know where you'll be sitting for the class period.

- Move the students around. Sometimes the seating arrangement is in a circle, sometimes in groups of four, sometimes in theatre-in-the-round style, sometimes in rows.

- Designate a "Critical Corner," where you stand to deliver important facts or information that the students really need to remember. When you stand there, the students' attention will be riveted on what you say because they know this is the main point of the lesson or facts that will show up later on a test.

- Try to include an activity that requires students to move around the room, if only to hand-deliver papers to your desk rather than passing them up.

- Even something as simple as having students stand when they know the answer breaks the routine and provides novelty.

Stay Informed

Read the article "Teaching for Creativity: Two Dozen Tips" (Sternberg & Williams, 1998) for great suggestions on how to implement creativity in your teaching. Suggestions include: modeling, encouraging idea generation, allowing time for creative thinking, encouraging sensible risks, tolerating ambiguity, allowing mistakes, identifying obstacles, encouraging creative collaboration, imagining others' viewpoints, finding excitement, and many others—not a bad list! Each of these topics is followed up by explanations and suggested actions for teachers to try out.

My 2009 book *Transformers: Creative Teachers for the 21st Century* is a resource for ideas, examples, and strategies to strengthen your creativity in the classroom. All the material has been teacher tested and can serve as a vehicle for engaging classes year after year.

Check out the Lincoln Center Institute's Capacities for Imaginative Learning (www.lcinstitute.org/wps/PA_1_0_P1/Docs/768-Ten-Capacities.pdf) for mega skills that underscore how universal imaginative learning should be. Are you employing any of these skills? Choose a few to work on.

Find Alternate Approaches

To nurture creative thinking, constantly remind your students to think of alternative ways to solve a problem. By doing this, you are switching your students' approach to looking at a problem from analytical to more divergent modes of thinking. Develop a habit of constantly asking, "Can you think of another way to approach this problem?" or "Why is this—or isn't this—the only way to figure out the answer?" You can always apply the mighty "What if?": What if you couldn't use a calculator for this problem? What if the war wasn't won by that country? What if you could no longer count on technology to handle communication?

Strengthen Students' Creative Muscles

Creativity needs to be practiced to become more readily accessible as a thinking tool. Most students become weaker in creative thinking as they move through our educational systems and with age. Being creatively fit is as important for our minds as being physically fit is for our bodies. Consider the following exercises to help strengthen your students' creative muscles:

- Set aside more time than usual for your students to really brainstorm ideas for a project or a writing assignment. We usually shortchange this opportunity for generating creative ideas. Explicitly point out the strengths of not settling for their first ideas but having an unlimited supply to pick from.

- Incorporate a "what if" question in each of your assignments. Get students in the habit of considering multiple implications of "what if" scenarios.

- Prove you value creative thinking by adding it as an element on every rubric you construct, every grade you give. Students will try to deliver what they perceive you value.

Reflection on Creativity

Did anything in this chapter echo your "first thoughts"? Which item(s) from the creativity baggy did you find relative to your own ideas on creativity? What forms of novelty do you already use in your teaching? How will you use creativity to engage and motivate your students? Formulate your own definition of creativity.

_____

_____

_____

_____

_____

_____

_____

_____

_____

_____

_____

_____

_____

_____

_____

One new strategy you might try out this week:

_____

Soft Skills

Each chapter of this book has represented a soft skill that teachers must possess to truly engage their students. Now we will look at how all these soft skills come together to create a balance and wisdom that defines the way of the teacher. We will also consider the soft skills of the students and how learning lessons from the past will help us to meet the needs of students in the future.

First Thoughts on Soft Skills

Think about the differences in obtaining cooperation by using force and by using love. Do you ever force students to do things that might not be in their best interests? Do you ever force students to do things you believe are in their best interests? Could there be another way?

Notes From the Field

I have a tattoo. It's the size of a nickel and on the heel of my right hand. If you don't look closely, you could easily think that a child drew on me with a couple of markers or that I let my hand rest on a wet page of a coloring book. I'm not the most likely person to be sporting a tattoo: I'm in my mid-sixties, a resident of a pretty conservative area in a very conservative state, a grandmother to thirteen children, and I spent the hippie revolution behind semi-cloistered, religious-order doors from 1962 to 1969. No, not your typical Bad Donkey Tattoo Parlor customer. But to my husband's utter amazement, I found it proper and fitting at this point in my life to have my flesh marked with a statement that I didn't want to let slip away, that I wanted to have dug into my psyche as well as my body.

My tattoo is an aleph (see fig. 12.1). The explanation of its meaning and form is taken from Itzhak Bentov's (2000) book *A Brief Tour of Higher Consciousness*. The aleph is pronounced "ah" and is the basic sound of the universe coming from the lungs unobstructed. Although the aleph is recognized by many as the first letter of the Hebrew alphabet, it is a far more ancient archetypal symbol embedded in human consciousness. It consists of three energy centers: the one on the left represents love; the one on the right represents will; the one in the center represents creation; and the sum of these three is wisdom. Each center radiates a different color symbolizing the quality of its energy frequency—gold for *love*, blue for *will*, red for *creation*—that together form the white light of wisdom.

Figure 12.1: Aleph.

Now here is the important part of this whole piece: in Hebrew, letters can be read from left to right or right to left, producing opposite meanings. If *will* is read from right to left toward *love*, it means destruction, extinction. But if read from *love* to *will*, it means to keep walking, to go. The cosmic law conveyed here is that if we go from love to will, we are all right and safe, but if we try to go from will to love, we are destroying the opportunity to manifest a love unencumbered by the force of our ego, a love that communicates a pure concern for another, free from a need to satisfy self. We must know love first. Love is the law of the cosmos.

So how does this apply to my life, you ask. Often we think we know what's best for people and try, with all apparent good intentions, to force our wills on them. While working with teachers and students, I've found that beginning with an attitude of love makes all the difference in how I view my work and how my work is accepted. The aleph reminds me to get rid of the "I know what's best for you" attitude and never force my will—or a school's will or a district's will—on teachers and students. This shift in perspective is a move away from the damaging overlay of force and toward fellowship and improvement. This perspective works. I don't ever want to forget this, thus the tattoo.

If we attempt to engage students in learning without first loving them, it won't work. We can't will them to be engaged. We must walk with them through the process, while nurturing them, building their confidence, offering choice and meaning, and challenging them. Loving our students will prompt us to ask, "What do my students need? How can I best fill those needs?" instead of, "How can I get them engaged in what I want them to do?"

The Discussion

The slow but steadily growing movement toward awareness of how we use our planet—toward dealing with our planet with a sense of love rather than force—is no longer a fringe issue. Climate changes, destruction of rain forests, massive landfill sites, air pollution, water scarcity and pollution, dangerous chemicals in our food, cancer-causing agents in everything from cooking utensils to medicines—everyone has at least a low level of awareness of these, along with a raft of other troubling reports on the condition of our environment.

There is another crisis, though, that is gaining public attention; along with our misuse of natural resources, we are experiencing a misuse or lack of use of human resources. Mentioned briefly earlier, Sir Kenneth Robinson, one of the foremost authorities on the need for creative and innovative thinking in 21st century classrooms, offers a powerful metaphor in describing schools' systematic failure to recognize much less nurture the multiple intelligences of our children. Robinson (2006) remarked during the TED presentation *Are Our Schools Killing Creativity?*:

> I believe our only hope for the future is to adopt a new conception of human ecology. One in which we start to reconstitute our conception of the richness of human capacity. Our education system

> has mined our minds in the way that we strip-mine the earth: for a particular commodity. And for the future it won't serve us. We have to rethink the fundamental principles upon which we are educating our children.

Here he likens the current education practices to the strip-mining of our children's minds for the purpose of extracting a single commodity rather than educating for a world that understands and develops the richness of human capacity. He goes on to say that we are essentially crushing individualism and creativity by making students aim for the system's idea of perfection, which seems to be "mini-professors." If we are trying, as Robinson asserts, to "educate children for a future we cannot grasp," it seems that we are "ruthlessly squandering" an opportunity to ignite their inherent creative capacities to deal with and shape that future.

Standards are good, even necessary, for quality achievement, but standards that are narrowly fixated on one type of intelligence at the expense of all the rest are harmful to children who possess the wide range of abilities, aptitudes, and gifts inherent in the intelligences that aren't associated with analytical thinking. Instead of school reform that tries to salvage the old system, we really need to look toward educational transformation that acknowledges and embraces the whole human organism. We need to look toward educational transformation that not only stresses reading, 'riting, and 'rithmatic, but also emphasizes three new Rs: reflection, relationship, and resilience, addressing the mind that is sadly underdeveloped and a wasted resource within our present system (Knapik, 2009). Here lies the heart of what is needed to entice students into that realm of engagement we so desire. A future more interested in nurturing and strengthening the organic abilities of our children will provide not only higher achievement scores in the present, but also adults capable of handling and coping with the complexities of their world in the long run.

Cicero prophetically wrote, "What a society does to its children, so will its children do to society." Consider what we are doing to our children in the name of higher test scores. What could this possibly imply about our future?

Balance, Above All

Healthy living is dependent on balance. Too much of a good thing simply isn't a good thing. Too little access to a necessity will eventually take its toll. A quick look at Maslow's hierarchy of needs—physiological, safety, love/belonging, esteem, and self-actualization (Maslow, 1954)—reminds us of the value of fulfilling children's basic needs before attempting to fill their heads with higher-order thinking exercises. But it takes a strong constitution to maintain the obvious in the face of pressure and social fears. One fear that is hampering the commonsense use of balance is the fear that children won't be prepared to be successful in meeting the demands of academic learning, and this fear is affecting our smallest students: our kindergarteners, even our preschoolers in some cases.

Against all research on human development and age-appropriate behaviors, schools are sliding the testing, teaching, and stress-creating processes of the upper grades down to the youngest members of our education factories. Studies conducted by researchers from UCLA, Long Island University, and Sarah Lawrence College documented in *Crisis in the Kindergarten: Why Children Need to Play in School* (Miller & Almon, 2009) found that:

- On a typical day, kindergartners in Los Angeles and New York City spend four to six times as long being instructed and tested in literacy and math (two to three hours per day) as in free play or "choice time" (thirty minutes or less).

- Standardized testing and preparation for tests are now daily activities in most of the kindergartens studied, despite the fact that the use of most such tests with children under age eight is scientifically invalid and leads to harmful labeling.

- In many kindergarten classrooms, there is no playtime at all. Teachers say the curriculum does not incorporate play and there isn't time for it, and many school administrators do not value it.

The research on the relationship between play and future cognitive development is dramatic. The *Crisis in the Kindergarten* report goes on to explain,

> Children who engage in complex forms of socio-dramatic play have greater language skills than non-players, better social skills, more empathy, more imagination, and more of the subtle capacity to know what others mean. They are less aggressive and show more self-control and higher levels of thinking. Long-term research casts doubt on the assumption that starting earlier on the teaching of phonics and other discrete skills leads to better results.

In support of these findings are the results of a long-term study released in 2008 by the Department of Education's research arm that found that students in schools using Reading First, which provides grants to improve elementary school reading, failed to score any better on comprehension tests than their peers who attended schools that did not receive Reading First money (Glod, 2008).

Test results of children under the age of eight are said to be as valid as flipping a coin, yet more and more schools are daily spending precious time preparing such students to take standardized tests. Even though no professional testing organization would ethically back the use of standardized tests alone to serve as a valid method of placing students in gifted or special education programs or determining retention or promotion, this is happening in some districts today. Therefore, parents are demanding that their children be prepared for the high-stakes tests that they believe will influence their children's entire school experience and chances for future success, and schools are bending to this pressure in spite of the research to the contrary that free, imaginative play is crucial for normal social, emotional, and cognitive development. If we want better adjusted, smarter, and less stressed young people, we will not teach them how to bubble in answers in the correct blocks, but rather how to blow bubbles from wands and make skyscrapers with blocks.

A related nightmare to this emphasis on early drill and study is the amount of work that is sent home for parents to do with their children. Reports of children—especially boys—fighting and resisting an extra hour of homework after having spent the entire day in such activities are growing from coast to coast. For instance, a comprehensive study by Julie Coates and William Draves (2006) confirms that boys are behind in school primarily because of difficulties in meeting teachers' homework requirements. If there is no room for play in the school day, and then the students are sent home with more schoolwork to do, when, if ever, does a five-year-old get the opportunity to play?

Those teaching the upper grades will not have an easy time—and more likely will have an impossible time—trying to engage students who have had nothing but an extended feeling of dread and possibly outright hatred for anything to do with school since they were babies. Math teachers in the upper grades will soon be dealing with the kindergarteners who cried weekly because they didn't want to take the numbers tests, who were building up a dislike and fear of math that was constructing an insurmountable wall of resentment. This is an example of "will before love" that will cause disruption in our educational efforts in the future.

Learning From the Past

A popular reason given for the study of history is to keep us from constantly repeating the same mistakes over and over. Another reason might be to examine what we did or thought in the past that wasn't a mistake but was, in fact, beneficial and produced good results. Perhaps a critical look at education's past can yield important information on ways to supplement the good things we are doing in education today to make them even more effective, to provide the weight of focus that can shift the scales to a more reasonable position of balance. A look at the upside of the one-room schoolhouse is such an example.

Many people in positions of power and influence today are products of the one-room schooling situation. Although they were not able to access technology, had limited materials, were constantly in earshot of lessons that were not meant for them, and were limited in social or extracurricular activities, they had distinct advantages over those in our current system:

- Students were able to learn everything they were ever taught again and again. Repetition—which is so difficult to make time for in today's classes and its lack of which accounts for a large portion of memory problems—was never an issue. Fourth-graders heard what they had learned in third, second, and first grades. They also heard what they would be learning in the years ahead.

- In this system, the mixed ages allowed for older students to help younger students, reinforcing their own knowledge as well. This wasn't an exercise in cooperative learning; it was cooperative learning by necessity. The teacher needed the help of the older students when he or she was occupied with other students.

- Instruction was customized to each student's needs. Today we call this differentiation.

- Students had ample time to select reading that piqued their interests. The little classroom library was a student's escape from the schoolhouse and a portal to worlds outside his or her limited community. With all our concern for reading in today's schools, overlooked again and again is the simple fact that reading improves with reading, not necessarily with an overemphasis on instruction on reading. The time set aside for actual individual reading in our schools has been shrinking considerably since the 1980s.

When you extend this idea of mixing age groups, you can see the benefits of utilizing the resources of our elder populations. Why not have schools set up next to retirement homes? Classrooms within those retirement homes can provide opportunities for the old to read and listen to the young read and talk. Here relationships—a key to deep engagement—could be knitted together.

Such a scenario exists now. Grace Living Center in Jenks, Oklahoma, is part nursing home, part school: two classrooms of roughly 60 prekindergarten and kindergarten students and 170 "grandmas" and "grandpas." With today's emphasis on reading proficiency, it seemed a good fit to build connections between the two groups with books. Book Buddies is a program that pairs rotating groups of residents and kindergartners to read to each other for thirty minutes several times a week. Since 2004, Jenks has tracked the number of entering first-graders whose reading skills are below grade level. Ten percent fewer Grace Living Center students have required reading intervention in the first grade than their peers at the local elementary school (Tulsa Initiative Blog, 2009). This is an example of innovative thinking, of creating a newer version of an older concept of relationships between old and young, and of the better utilization of human resources. In other words, this is an example of love moving toward will with the result of creating wisdom.

A Picture of the Present

Much of the time spent on preparing students to score well on high-stakes tests runs counter to the growing consensus for the need for 21st century skills—survival skills that will develop children's abilities to cope and succeed in the future—to serve as the benchmarks for education. In one hand, we hold up models of innovation and call for creative thinking skills to be taught alongside analytical thinking skills. In the other hand, we hold up more stringent requirements for our children to reach testing proficiencies over a narrow band of intelligences.

We read reports of districts dropping the arts, electives, and physical education and opting for more test-preparation classes—squeezing out anything that can't be bubbled onto an answer sheet. We distill educational reform down to the metaphor of a race, which dictates that only a few win and the majority see themselves as losers. In spite of no known legitimate research in support, kindergarteners are stripped of their opportunity to play and instead are set upon a path of testing and homework. The need for our children to be fluent in using divergent as well as critical thinking is being thwarted by a growing culture intent on constantly seeking "the right" answer:

> Humans have survived for thousands of years by trying out new things, not by always getting the "right" tried and true answer. That's not healthy for growing a smart, adaptive brain. The notion of narrowed standardized tests to get the right answer violates the law of adaptiveness in a developing brain. Good quality education encourages the exploration of alternate thinking, multiple answers, and creative insights. (Jensen, 2009, p. 16)

Teacher Input

Reading First, mentioned briefly earlier, is a $6 billion federal reading program mandated under the No Child Left Behind Act. Schools funded by the program must use "scientifically based" reading instruction. A 2008 U.S. government report reveals that students involved in this program are not reading any better than those who don't participate (Glod, 2008). The fact that only one member of the National Reading Panel responsible for making the decision to adopt this program, Joanne Yatvin, had taught reading in a classroom setting should have sent up a red flag indicating that not enough input was being offered or received from those people who have had the most experience with reading instruction—teachers.

Outvoted and disregarded, Yatvin (2000) authored a report explaining that Reading First requires "explicit, systematic instruction," meaning that any skill or body of information is divided into discrete, step-by-step lessons to be learned by rote. Instructors present the objective of each lesson, principles, process, and some examples of application. Students memorize these elements and practice by applying them in controlled situations. Practice continues until students can apply the principles or the process correctly on their own. Yatvin (2007) points out that the problem with this type of instruction is that it does not square with what we know about how children learn:

> Decades of research on children's learning show that children tend to be random, concrete, piecemeal learners. Children do not start learning anything by rules and systematic steps. They experience concrete examples of phenomena, draw what they think are the principles from them, and then experiment by creating their own examples. If the created examples work, children accept their original principles; if not, they adjust them and try again. (p. 27)

Not only were those closest to the work of teaching barely allowed to offer their expertise before a billion-dollar effort at changing learning across the United States began, but she who was closest to the work of teaching and the sole voice invited to the table wasn't listened to.

Our voices as teachers are legitimate voices on matters that concern policy issues in education; we are the experts. We need to make our voices heard through whatever venues are accessible to us as professionals. This begins at the classroom level, where we participate in opportunities to meet and share our experiences with parents and district personnel. From there, it moves to our awareness of and contributions to local political discussions and races for office. In today's world, we can't assume that someone else will take over the role of advocate for us. List ways that you can advocate your beliefs and values in education from your personal circle (home) to professional circles (school, district) to even wider circles (community and political representatives).

Student Input

The greatest impact of any reform effort is on the students themselves. Asking students how they are handling the reform and listening to what they have to say might just be the last thought of those attempting to move this giant complex of education forward in a meaningful direction, but it might be one of the best.

Many students in the upper grades feel that there isn't anyone who will really listen to or consider what they have to say and that any efforts to state their opinions are useless. The HSSSE received 42,754 completed surveys from students from 103 high schools located in 27 states in 2008. Question 35 of those surveys asked, "Would you like to say more about any of your answers to these survey questions?" Responses were along the lines of the following:

- These surveys are pointless because you guys will do nothing even if there is a problem.

- Pointless! You won't change anyway, so why do you care?

- These surveys are pointless because no matter what we say none of the supervisors will listen to us.

- Do you really think a survey will change anything about this school?

- I do not believe anyone will read this and actually care.

- Will this survey change anything? Will curriculum be changed if enough people say they are bored? Will research papers be cut?

- Most of our teachers are great, but some that I've had are not. One didn't even know my name at the end of the year!

- Listen to the students and take us seriously! (Yazzie-Mintz, 2009)

The Way of the Teacher

How much have we learned from asking? From listening? From listening without an attachment to our predetermined ideas of what would be good for our students? Such an approach exemplifies love first and will second, merging into the creation of a better situation in which engagement is not only possible, but is the motivating force toward improved achievement. Many still don't believe this, though, and feel that force, punishment, and controlling environments are the answers to our educational problems.

The focus on ways to improve student achievement has been moving from forming assessments to building data banks, to formulating standards, to updating curricula, to implementing programs, and finally to investigating what determines quality teachers. Assuming that a teacher possesses the hard skills of the profession—knows the subject matter, knows the pedagogy of teacher education—the effective teacher with engaged students is the one with a mastery of a wide range of soft skills: the commonsense skills, the people skills, the skills that make an effective communicator. Although most highly sought after, these skills are not taught and seldom mentioned in schools as important.

An effective teacher must possess a few innate qualities that are seldom identified by recruiting and hiring practices, such as the abilities to trust, to withhold judgment, to listen with an open heart, to stay detached from personal opinions and agendas, to maintain a sense of humor, and to remain flexible. Angeles Arrien (2001), in her essay "The Way of the Teacher," defines the opposite of trust as an attempt to control the uncontrollable. She says that "an individual who has difficulty with surprises or the unexpected has attachments, fixed perspectives, and a strong need for control" (p. 152). She goes on to make the point that here the word *attachment* does not apply to owning and wanting to hold on to things but rather to hold on to immovable expectations, desires that are projected onto people, places, and situations. These types of attachments make us controlling and rigid. Arrien suggests that when we observe what makes us lose our sense of humor, we can identify our point of attachment and stretch ourselves to begin letting go of those attitudes and ideas that make us rigid. Student engagement is often contingent on whether students observe in their teacher an attitude of acceptance of the ideas and opinions they voice in class.

In most traditional societies, the common perception of the way of the teacher is the way of wisdom. It is no coincidence that the fusing together of love, will, and creation on my little aleph results in wisdom. Wisdom lies in the acknowledgment of and meshing together of a teacher's hard and soft skills.

Steps Toward Solutions

> *The good teacher starts with where her or his students*
> *are, and leads them to where they should be—in terms of*
> *understandings and values.*
>
> —Howard Gardner

Throughout these exercises, you will be asked to evaluate the use and effectiveness of soft skills in your past and present experiences as a teacher. By identifying the soft skills in your own practice, you will be in a position to accentuate their use for better results in bolstering student engagement.

Evaluate Past Educational Trends

Make a historical time line of educational trends that have affected you as a student as well as a teacher (for example, the implementation of quarter courses or the dropping of required courses, themed units of study, the trend of the open classroom where walls were torn down in school buildings and space was given to each class, the trend toward whole-language reading or new-math initiatives, and so on).

Evaluate each trend as either effective or ineffective—or even damaging. What made some trends valuable, and what made others fade out quickly? Are there any aspects of those past trends that could benefit us today if embedded in our current educational methods?

Show That You Care

Your impact on the students who walk into your classroom day after day, year after year, is profound and lasting, and your actions are capable of making or breaking a student's spirit. Often the quality of your impact is gauged by the caring you display—for yourself, for your students, for your subject matter. Nel Noddings, a renowned educator and author of *The Challenge to Care in Schools,* states:

> Education should be organized around themes of care rather than traditional disciplines. All students should emerge in a general education that guides them in caring for self, intimate others, global others, plants, animals, and the environment, the human-made world and ideas. Such an aim doesn't work against intellectual development or academic achievement. On the contrary, it supplies a firm foundation for both. (as quoted in Lantieri, 2001, p. 169)

With Noddings's words in mind, answer the following questions:

- Discuss with another how caring could actually provide a firm foundation for "intellectual development or academic achievement." Does this emphasis on caring have any bearing on why you entered the field of education in the first place? How?

- If you ran into students whom you taught more than a decade ago, what would you like them to tell you about your teaching and what they remember from your class? Write down a paragraph or two of what you would like them to say.

- What characteristics are necessary in a teacher's interaction with students to *make* instead of *break* their spirits? List them.

- Pretend a student or peer asks you why you became a teacher and why you have chosen to stay a teacher. Write down how you would answer.

Maintain a Sense of Humor

Do you believe that when people look back on their most influential teachers, one of the top characteristics they remember is sense of humor? A sense of humor is indeed one of the soft skills most appreciated by students. Write down a few incidents from your own schooling and from your own teaching during which a sense of humor was especially valuable. Describe the teachers you remember for their sense of humor.

Communicate Your Hopes for Your Students

Angeles Arrien, in *Schools With Spirit: Nurturing the Inner Lives of Children and Teachers* (Lantieri, 2001), writes a poignant "Invocation for the Children of the Future" that includes thirteen statements beginning with the words *May you*. The first two read:

> May you be powerfully loving and lovingly powerful; may you always have love be your guide with your family, friends, and colleagues. Remember to listen carefully to your own heart and to the hearts of others.
>
> May you have the courage to always follow your dreams. Take an action every day to support your life dream, your love of nature, and your integrity. (p. 170)

I'm sure you can think of many other statements that could communicate your hopes and desires for your students' futures. Try the following suggestions to put these feelings into words:

1. Write a set of "May you . . ." statements that you would wish for the children of the future.

2. Go to www.family-connection.org/invocation.htm to read the rest of Arrien's thirteen wishes, and add any to your list that you feel are particularly important.

3. Type your list and tape it to the inside of your planning book to remind you of what you really want for your students' futures. Remember that your thoughts today frame and manifest the reality of the future.

Create a Student Survey

Make up your own survey to get your students' thoughts on whether they feel engaged in school and why or why not:

1. Ask your students for input on the survey questions.

2. View the HSSSE at www.indiana.edu/~ceep/hssse for inspiration.

3. Involve your fellow teachers in building this survey.

4. Use the results as the basis for a faculty discussion, a class discussion, and input for professional development planning.

5. As a result of a student comment or response, make a change within your school—empower your students by showing them that their voices are being heard and acted upon.

6. Discuss the power to be had by listening to dissenting voices and not simply to those who agree with the persons in charge. Act on this understanding in your classroom.

Reflection on Soft Skills

Soft skills allow us to use our expertise as educators more effectively and to show a respectful love for those with whom we work and those we teach. List the soft skills you possess and explain how they can be used to engage your students.

_____

_____

_____

_____

_____

_____

_____

_____

_____

_____

_____

_____

_____

_____

One new strategy you might try out this week:

_____

Rank the Soft Skills

The following table lists soft skills. Mark all those that are important for teachers to possess. Choose the top five from those you have marked and explain why each is a necessary skill. Go through the list again from the perspective of your students— which five do you think they would mark as most important for you to possess?

Soft Skills	Important to You	Important to Your Students	Explanation of Top Five Soft Skills
Ability to think creatively			
Ability to recognize teaching as an art			
Ability to set goals			
Ability to manage anger			
Ability to cope with adverse situations			
Ability to maintain withitness			
Ability to explain ideas and break down complexities			
Ability to influence emotional states			
Ability to effectively interview another			
Ability to make good decisions			
Ability to solve problems			
Ability to read body language			
Ability to delegate and build a team			
Ability to appropriately convey emotion			
Ability to maintain a sense of humor			

Page 1 of 2

Soft Skills	Important to You	Important to Your Students	Explanation of Top Five Soft Skills
Ability to negotiate			
Ability to resolve conflict			
Ability to manage time			
Ability to be assertive			
Ability to effectively communicate			
Ability to inspire others			
Ability to express oneself			
Ability to actively listen			
Ability to build rapport			
Ability to innovate			
Ability to manage stress			
Ability to develop cultural awareness			
Ability to make small talk			
Ability to convey empathy and communicate caring			
Ability to remain positive			
Ability to bolster confidence			

Page 2 of 2

References and Resources

Alexie, S. (2009). *The absolutely true diary of a part-time Indian*. New York: Little, Brown and Company.

Amabile, T. M. (1985, February). Motivation and creativity: Effects of motivational orientation on creative writers. *Journal of Personality and Social Psychology, 48*(2), 393–399.

Anderson, L. W., & Krathwohl, D. R. (Eds.). (2001). *A taxonomy for learning, teaching and assessing: A revision of Bloom's taxonomy of educational objectives*. New York: Longman.

Anderson, L. W., & Sosniak, L. A. (Eds.). (1994). *Bloom's taxonomy: A forty-year retrospective. Ninety-third yearbook of the National Society for the Study of Education* (Pt. 2). Chicago: University of Chicago Press.

Ardagh, A. (2005). *The translucent revolution: How people just like you are waking up and changing the world*. Novato, CA: New World Library.

Arrien, A. (2001). The way of the teacher. In L. Lantieri (Ed.), *Schools with spirit: Nurturing the inner lives of children and teachers* (pp. 148–157). Boston: Beacon Press.

Barsade, S. G. (2002, December). The ripple effect: Emotional contagion and its influence on group behavior. *Administrative Science Quarterly, 47*(4), 644–675. Accessed at www.jstor.org/pss/3094912 on June 11, 2010.

Baylor, B. (1995). *I'm in charge of celebrations*. New York: Alladin Paperbacks.

Beers, K. (2009, March). *The genteel unteaching of America's poor*. Urbana, IL: National Council of Teachers of English.

Beilock, S. L., Gunderson, E. A., Ramirez, G., & Levine, S. C. (2010, February 2). Female teachers' math anxiety affects girls' math achievement. *Proceedings of the National Academy of Sciences, 107*(5), 1860–1863.

Bentov, I. (2000). *A brief tour of higher consciousness*. Rochester, VT: Destiny Books.

Black, P., & Wiliam, D. (1998a). Assessment and classroom learning. *Assessment in Education: Principles, Policy & Practice, 5*(1), 7–74.

Black, P., & Wiliam, D. (1998b). Inside the black box: Raising standards through classroom assessment. *Phi Delta Kappan, 80*(2), 139–148. Accessed at www.pdkintl.org/kappan/kbla9810.htm on January 3, 2010.

Blackwell, L. S., Trzesniewski, K. H., & Dweck, C. S. (2007). Implicit theories of intelligence predict achievement across an adolescent transition: A longitudinal study and an intervention. *Child Development, 78*(1), 246–263.

Blum, R. W., McNeely, C. A., & Rinehart, P. M. (2002). *Improving the odds: The untapped power of schools to improve the health of teens.* Minneapolis: Center for Adolescent Health and Development, University of Minnesota.

Boehlert, M. (2005). Self-fulfilling prophecy. In S. W. Lee (Ed.), *Encyclopedia of school psychology.* Thousand Oaks, CA: Sage.

Bradford, W. C. (2004). Reaching the visual learner: Teaching property through art. *The Law Teacher, 11.* Accessed at http://ssrn.com/abstract=587201 on August 24, 2010.

Brewster, C., & Fager, J. (2000). *Increasing student engagement and motivation: From time-on-task to homework.* Portland, OR: Northwest Regional Educational Laboratory. Accessed at www.nwrel.org/request/oct00/textonly.html on July 25, 2009.

Bruner, J. (1965). The growth of mind. *American Psychologist, 20,* 1007–1017.

Burns, T., & Sinfield, S. (2004). *Teaching, learning and study skills: A guide for tutors.* Thousand Oaks, CA: Sage Publications Ltd.

Caine, G., & Caine, R. N. (2001). *The brain, education and the competitive edge.* Lanham, MD: ScarecrowEducation.

Caine, G., & Caine, R. N. (2009). *The Natural Learning Research Institute grounded in the system principles of natural learning.* Accessed at www.naturallearning institute.org/UPDATEDSITE/RESEARCHFOUNDATION/Understanding Learning.html on October 7, 2009.

Caine Learning Center. (2010). *How people learn: Grounded in the 12 brain/mind learning principles.* Accessed at www.cainelearning.com/files/Learning.html on August 26, 2010.

Caine, R. N., & Caine, G. (1994). *Making connections: Teaching and the human brain.* Palo Alto, CA: Dale Seymour Publications.

Caine, R. N., Caine, G., McClintic, C., & Klimek, K. (2008). *The 12 brain/mind learning principles in action.* Twelve Oaks, CA: Corwin Press.

Cameron, J. (2002). *The artist's way: A spiritual path to higher creativity.* New York: Jeremy P. Tarcher/Putnam.

Carey, B. (2009, April 16). Task to aid self-esteem lifts grades for some. *New York Times*. Accessed at www.nytimes.com/2009/04/17/science/17esteem .html?_r=3&ref=education on September 15, 2009.

Carlsson-Paige, N. (2001). Nurturing meaningful connections with young children. In L. Lantieri (Ed.), *Schools with spirit: Nurturing the inner lives of children and teachers* (pp. 21–38). Boston, MA: Beacon Press.

Centers for Disease Control and Prevention. (2009). *School connectedness: Strategies for increasing protective factors among youth*. Atlanta: U.S. Department of Health and Human Services.

Coates, J., & Draves, W. (2006). Smart boys, bad grades. Accessed at www .smartboysbadgrades.com on August 30, 2010.

Cody, A. (2009, December 31). Dr. Atkin: Formative assessment is not test preparation. [Blog entry]. Accessed at http://blogs.edweek.org/teachers/living-in -dialogue/ on January 3, 2010.

Cooper, H. M. (1979). Pygmalion grows up: A model for teacher expectation communication and performance influence. *Review of Educational Research*, *49*(3), 389–410.

Cooper, H. M., & Tom, D. (1984). Teacher expectation research: A review with implications for classroom instruction. *Elementary School Journal*, *85*(1), 76–89.

Corno, L., & Winne, P. H. (Eds.). (2002, Spring). Emotions in education [Special issue]. *Educational Psychologist*, *37*(2).

Costa, A., & Kallick, B. (2009). *Learning and leading with habits of mind: Sixteen essential characteristics for success*. Alexandria, VA: Association for Supervision and Curriculum Development.

Csikszentmihalyi, M. (1991). Thoughts about education. *New Horizons for Learning*. Accessed at www.newhorizons.org/future/Creating_the_Future/crfut_csikszent .html on August 24, 2010.

Csikszentmihalyi, M. (2008). *Flow: The psychology of optimal experience (P.S.)*. New York: Harper Perennial Modern Classics.

Cullen, C. C. (2005). *List of emotions*. Accessed at www.mytherapistnc.org/emotions .htm on January 15, 2010.

David, J. L. (2008, February). Project-based learning: Teaching students to think. *Educational Leadership*, *65*(5), 80–82.

Davis, B. M. (2006). *How to teach students who don't look like you: Culturally relevant teaching strategies*. Thousand Oaks, CA: Corwin Press.

Davis, B. M. (2008). *How to coach teachers who don't think like you: Using literacy strategies to coach across content areas.* Thousand Oaks, CA: Corwin Press.

Davis, B. M. (2009). *The biracial and multiracial student experience: A journey to racial literacy.* Thousand Oaks, CA: Corwin Press.

de Bono, E. (1992). *Serious creativity: Using the power of lateral thinking to create new ideas.* New York: HarperBusiness.

Deci, E. (1985, March). The well-tempered classroom. *Psychology Today, 19*(3), 52–53.

Deci, E., & Ryan, M. (1985). *Intrinsic motivation and self-determination in human behavior.* New York: Plenum.

Diamond, M., & Hopson, J. (1999). *Magic trees of the mind: How to nurture your child's intelligence, creativity, and healthy emotions from birth through adolescence.* New York: Plume.

Dweck, C. (2008). *Mindset: The new psychology of success.* New York: Ballantine Books.

Equity Training and Development Team. (2007). *Proximity.* Accessed at www.montgomeryschoolsmd.org/departments/development/teams/diversity/diversity.shtm on December 13, 2009.

Equity Training and Development Team. (2008). *The teacher uses body language, gestures, and expressions.* Accessed at www.montgomeryschoolsmd.org/departments/development/teams/diversity/diversity.shtm on December 13, 2009.

Equity Training and Development Team. (2009). *A resource for equitable classroom practices, 2009.* Accessed at www.montgomeryschoolsmd.org/departments/development/documents/ECP%20-%2009–30–09.pdf on January 6, 2010.

Evans, S., & Ardill, M. (1999, April 25). Relax, it's just black. *Toronto Star,* pp. D16–D17.

Fixsen, D. L., Naoom, S. F., Blase, K. A., Friedman, R. M., & Wallace, F. (2005). *Implementation research: A synthesis of the literature.* Tampa, FL: University of South Florida, Louis de la Parte Florida Mental Health Institute, The National Implementation Research Network.

Fletcher, R. (2006). *Boy writers: Reclaiming their voices.* Portland, ME: Stenhouse Publishers; Markham, Ontario, Canada: Pembroke Publishers.

Forehand, M. (2005). Bloom's taxonomy: Original and revised. In M. Orey (Ed.), *Emerging perspectives on learning, teaching, and technology.* Accessed at http://projects.coe.uga.edu/epltt/ on August 12, 2010.

Gallo, C. (2009). *The presentation secrets of Steve Jobs: How to be insanely great in front of any audience* [Slideshow presentation]. Accessed at www.slideshare.net/cvgallo/the-presentation-secrets-ofstevejobs2609477?utm_source=MailingList&utm_medium=email&utm_content=marykim%40aol.com&utm_campaign=Newsletter+2009+Dec+3 on January 5, 2010.

Gardner, H. (2008). *Five minds for the future*. Boston: Harvard Business Press.

Gay, G. (2000). *Culturally responsive teaching*. New York: Teachers College Press.

Gleason, R. (2007). "Building stronger relationships" (pp. 72–75). Unpublished case study written at the International Education Consortium's Missouri Humanities Program in St. Louis, MO.

Glod, M. (2008, May 2). Study questions "No Child" Act's reading plan: Lauded program fails to improve test scores. *Washington Post*. Accessed at www.washingtonpost.com/wpdyn/content/article/2008/05/01/AR2008050101399.html on January 8, 2010.

Goleman, D. (1991, October 15). Happy or sad, a mood can prove contagious. *New York Times*. Accessed at www.nytimes.com/1991/10/15/science/happy-or-sad-a-mood-can-prove-contagious.html?pagewanted=2 on August 24, 2010.

Goleman, D. (1995). *Emotional intelligence: Why it can matter more than IQ*. New York: Bantam Books.

Good, T. (1987). Two decades of research on teacher expectations and future direction. *Journal of Teacher Education, 38*(4), 32–47.

Good, T., & Brophy, J. (1987). *Looking in classrooms* (4th ed.). New York: Harper & Row.

Good, T., & Brophy, J. (2000). *Looking in classrooms* (8th ed.). New York: Longman.

Gordon, L. (1999). *52 ways to nurture your creativity*. San Francisco: Chronicle Books.

Guthrie, C. (2008). Mind over matters through meditation. *O, the Oprah Magazine*. Accessed at www.oprah.com/article/omagazine/200812_omag_meditate on January 6, 2010.

Harmel, K. (1999, January 25). Teachers' nonverbal clues affect students' performance. *ScienceDaily*. Accessed at www.sciencedaily.com/releases/1999/01/990122130911.htm on November 10, 2009.

Hattie, J. (1992). Measuring the effects of schooling. *Australian Journal of Education, 36*(1), 5–13.

Heylighen, F., Joslyn, C., & Turchin, V. (Eds.). (1999, February 19). Change and information overload: Negative effects. *Principia Cybernetica Web*. Accessed at http://cleamc11.vub.ac.be/chinneg.html on June 11, 2010.

Huitt, W. (2001). Motivation to learn: An overview. Educational Psychology Interactive. Accessed at www.edpsycinteractive.org/col/motivation/motivate .html on August 24, 2010.

Hunter, P. A. (2009). *Breaking the mould: True stories about ordinary people becoming powerful*. Loch Long, Scotland: Librario Publishing Ltd.

Ito, M., Carter, M., & Thorne, B. (2008). *Digital youth research: Kids' informal learning with digital media*. The John D. and Catherine T. MacArthur Foundation. Accessed at http://digitalyouth.ischool.berkeley.edu/report on January 5, 2010.

Ito, M., Horst, H. A., Bittanti, M., Boyd, D., Herr-Stephenson, B., Lange, P., Pascoe, C. J., & Robinson, L. (2008, November). *Living and learning with new media: Summary of findings from the digital youth project*. Accessed at http://digitalyouth.ischool.berkeley.edu/files/report/digitalyouth-WhitePaper .pdf on August 26, 2010.

Jackson, R. R. (2009). *Never work harder than your students and other principles of great teaching*. Alexandria, VA: Association for Supervision and Curriculum Development.

Jackson, R. R. (2010). Start where your students are. *Educational Leadership, 67*(5), 6–10.

Jensen, E. (2000). *Learning with the body in mind*. Thousand Oaks, CA: Corwin Press.

Jensen, E. (2003). *Tools for engagement: Managing emotional states for learner success*. San Diego: The Brain Store.

Jensen, E. (2009). *Teaching with poverty in mind: What being poor does to kids' brains and what schools can do about it*. Alexandria, VA: Association for Supervision and Curriculum Development.

Jeurling, C. (Producer). (2007, December 10). *Phorecast Podcast No 01—Sir Ken Robinson* [Audio podcast]. Accessed at http://cdn3.libsyn.com/voccine /phorecast_01.mp3?nvb=20100107143533&nva=20100108144533&t=0d 71d87e5920a4eb92f69 on January 6, 2010.

Jones, C. (1991). *Mistakes that worked*. New York: Delacorte Press.

Jones, F. (2000). *Tools for teaching: Discipline, instruction, motivation*. Santa Cruz, CA: Fredric H. Jones & Associates, Inc.

Jones, F. (2003). Effective room arrangement. *Education World*. Accessed at www
.education-world.com/a_curr/columnists/jones/jones001.shtml on June 11,
2010.

Kahneman, D. (2010, February 10). *The riddle of experience vs. memory.*
Presentation given at TED2010, Long Beach, CA. Accessed at www.ted
.com/talks/daniel_kahneman_the_riddle_of_experience_vs_memory.html
on June 11, 2010.

Kaufman, B. (1965). *Up the down staircase.* Englewood Cliffs, NJ: Prentice-Hall, Inc.

Klem, A. M., & Connell, J. P. (2004). Relationships matter: Linking teacher support
to student engagement and achievement. *Journal of School Health*, 74(7),
262–273.

Knapik, M. (2009, October 19). *Feeling "Blue" about education never seemed so
hopeful* [Blog entry]. Accessed at http://blog.grdodge.org/2009/10/19
/feeling-blue-about-education-never-seemed-so-hopeful/ on August 26, 2010.

Kounin, J. (1970). *Discipline and group management in classrooms.* New York:
Holt, Rinehart and Winston.

Kroft, S. (Writer), Klug, R., & Flaum, A. T. (Directors). (2010). Watching the border:
The virtual fence. In K. Sharman (Producer), *60 Minutes*. Accessed at
www.cbsnews.com/stories/2010/01/07/60minutes/main6067598.shtml on
July 6, 2010.

Lamott, A. (1995). *Bird by bird.* New York: Anchor Books.

Land, G., & Jarman, B. (1998). *Breakpoint and beyond: Mastering the future today.*
Scottsdale, AZ: Leadership 2000 Inc.

Langan, P. (2002). *The bully.* West Berlin, NJ: Townsend Press.

Lantieri, L. (Ed.). (2001). *Schools with spirit: Nurturing the inner lives of children
and teachers.* Boston: Beacon Press.

Lengel, T., & Kuczala, M. (Eds.). (2010). *The kinesthetic classroom: Teaching and
learning through movement.* Thousand Oaks, CA: Corwin Press.

Levin, J., & Nolan, J. F. (2002). *What every teacher should know about classroom
management.* Boston: Allyn & Bacon.

Levine, A. (2009). *50 web 2.0 ways to tell a story.* Accessed at http://cogdogroo
.wikispaces.com/StoryTools on January 13, 2010.

Lindsey, R. B., Robins, K. N., & Terrell, R. D. (2003). *Cultural proficiency: A manual
for school leaders.* Thousand Oaks, CA: Corwin Press.

Liu, E., & Noppe-Brandon, S. (2009). *Imagination first: Unlocking the power of possibility*. San Francisco: Jossey-Bass.

Lynne, K., Lane, M., Pierson, R., & Givner, C. (2003). Teacher expectations of student behavior: Which skills do elementary and secondary teachers deem necessary for success in the classroom? *Education & Treatment of Children*, *26*(4), 413–430. Accessed at www.questia.com/googleScholar .qst?docId=5002063677 on December 17, 2009.

Marsh, L. (2009, October). Spend some of that $650 million for educational video games. Accessed at http://voices.kansascity.com/node/6135/ on October 8, 2009.

Marshall, K. (2009, July 29). Are schools wounding kids? *Teacher Magazine*. Accessed at www.teachermagazine.org/tm/articles/2009/07/29/tln30_marshall.h21 .html?tkn=NOMD8%2B7hiyi7gi9lHxh9U7iV%2BnBdzFxK4jlW&print=1 on July 30, 2009.

Marzano, R. J., Pickering, D. J., & Pollock, J. E. (2001). *Classroom instruction that works: Research-based strategies for increasing student achievement*. Alexandria, VA: Association for Supervision and Curriculum Development.

Maslow, A. (1954). *Motivation and personality*. New York: Harper.

McTighe, J., & Seif, E. (2003, November). A summary of underlying theory and research for understanding by design. *Manitoba Association for Supervision and Curriculum Development*, *11*(1), 6–16.

Medina, J. (2009). *Brain rules: 12 principles for surviving and thriving at work, home, and school*. Seattle, WA: Pear Press.

Mehrabian, A. (1969). *Silent messages*. Belmont, CA: Wadsworth Publishing Co.

Mendler, A. N. (2000). *Motivating students who don't care: Successful techniques for educators*. Bloomington, IN: Solution Tree Press.

MetLife. (2009). *The MetLife survey of the American teacher: Collaborating for student success, part two: Student achievement*. New York: Author.

Meyer, D. K., & Turner, J. C. (2002). Discovering emotion in classroom motivation research. *Educational Psychologist*, *37*(2), 107–114.

Miller, E., & Almon, J. (2009). *Crisis in the kindergarten: Why children need to play in school*. College Park, MD: Alliance for Childhood. Accessed at http:// drupal6.allianceforchildhood.org/sites/allianceforchildhood.org/files/file /kindergarten_report.pdf on January 8, 2010.

Miller, P. W. (2005). Body language in the classroom. *Techniques: Connecting Education and Careers*, *80*(8), 28–30.

Mintzer, M. Z., & Snodgrass, J. G. (1999). The picture superiority effect: Support for the distinctiveness model. *American Journal of Psychology, 112*, 113–146.

Montagne, R. (Host). (2007, July 9). Study: Virtual games hone real business skills. On *Morning Edition*. Washington, DC: National Public Radio. Accessed at www.npr.org/templates/story/story.php?storyId=11823637 on December 29, 2009.

Moore, R. (2010, March 13). Yes, they can [Blog entry]. Accessed at http:// teacherleaders.typepad.com/teachmoore/2010/03/yes-they-can.html on August 24, 2010.

Morris, W. (2006). *Creativity: Its place in education*. Accessed at www.jpb.com /creative/Creativity_in_Education.pdf on February 12, 2009.

Mottel, T., & Beebe, S. (2000). *Emotional contagion in the classroom: An examination of how teacher and student emotions are related*. Accessed at www .eric.ed.gov/PDFS/ED447522.pdf on August 24, 2010.

Olson, K. (2009). *Wounded by school: Recapturing the joy in learning and standing up to old school culture*. New York: Teachers College Press.

Omaha Public Schools. (2005). *Teacher's corner: Comprehension: Bloom's taxonomy*. Accessed at www.ops.org/reading/blooms_taxonomy.html on March 21, 2009.

Payne, R. K. (2005). *A framework for understanding poverty*. Highlands, TX: aha! Process, Inc.

Pert, C. (2006). *Everything you need to know to feel go(o)d*. Carlsbad, CA: Hay House, Inc.

Pink, D. (2009, July 24). *The surprising science of motivation*. Presentation given at TEDGlobal 2009, Oxford, UK. Accessed at http://blog.ted.com/2009/08 /the_surprising.php on October 26, 2009.

Pink, D. H. (2005). *A whole new mind: Moving from the information age into the conceptual age*. Crows Nest, New South Wales, Australia: Allen & Unwin.

Prensky, M. (2006). *Don't bother me, mom—I'm learning!* St. Paul, MN: Paragon House Publishers.

Renninger, K. A., Hidi, S., & Krapp, A. (Eds.). (1992). *The role of interest in learning and development*. Hillsdale, NJ: Erlbaum.

Resseger, J. (2009). *My learning story*. Accessed at http://rethinklearningnow.com /stories/story/?storyId=29726 on November 23, 2009.

Rethink Learning Now. (n.d.). Share your voice. Accessed at http://rethinklearningnow .com/stories/submit/ on February 7, 2010.

Richards, S. (2007). The last word: An interview with Arthur L. Costa. *Journal of Advanced Academics*. Accessed at http://goliath.ecnext.com/coms2/gi_0199–6849173/The-last-word-an-interview.html on October 24, 2009.

Ripley, A. (2010). What makes a great teacher? *Atlantic, 305*(1), 58–66.

Risley, T. R., & Hart, B. (1995). *Meaningful differences in the everyday experience of young American children.* Baltimore, MD: Paul H. Brookes Publishing Co.

Robins, K. N., Lindsey, R. B., Lindsey, D. B., & Terrell, R. D. (2002). *Culturally proficient instruction: A guide for people who teach.* Thousand Oaks, CA: Corwin Press.

Robinson, K. (2006, February 23). *Are our schools killing creativity?* Presentation given at TED2006, Monterey, CA. Accessed at www.ted.com/talks/lang/eng/ken_robinson_says_schools_kill_creativity.html on January 9, 2009.

Robinson, K. (2009). *The element: How finding your passion changes everything.* New York: Penguin.

Rodriguez, E. R., & Bellanca, J. (2007). *What is it about me you can't teach? An instructional guide for the urban educator.* Thousand Oaks, CA: Corwin Press.

Roschelle, J., Penuel, W. R., & Abrahamson, L. (2004). *Classroom response and communication systems: Research review and theory.* Paper presented at the Annual Meeting of the American Educational Research Association, San Diego, CA.

Rosenthal, R. (1968). *Pygmalion in the classroom.* New York: Holt, Rinehart and Winston.

Ryan, R. M., & Deci, E. L. (2000, January). Self-determination theory and the facilitation of intrinsic motivation, social development, and well-being. *American Psychologist, 55*(1), 68–78.

Scheffler, I. (1991). *In praise of the cognitive emotions: And other essays in the philosophy of education.* New York: Routledge, Chapman and Hall, Inc.

Schmoker, M. (2001, October 24). The "Crayola curriculum." *Education Week.* Accessed at http://mikeschmoker.com/crayola-curriculum.html on December 10, 2009.

Schmoker, M. (2006). *Results now: How we can achieve unprecedented improvements in teaching and learning.* Alexandria, VA: Association for Supervision and Curriculum Development.

Schreck, M. K. (2007). *Body language: Poems from the inside out.* Columbia, MO: Tigress Press.

Schreck, M. K. (2009). *Transformers: Creative teachers for the 21st century.* Thousand Oaks, CA: Corwin Press.

Shernoff, D., Csikszentmihalyi, M., Schneider, B., & Shernoff, E. (2003). Student engagement in high school classrooms from the perspective of flow theory. *School Psychology Quarterly, 18*(2), 158–176.

Shernoff, D. J., & Csikszentmihalyi, M. (2009). Flow in schools: Cultivating engaged learners and optimal learning environments. In R. Gilman, E. S. Huebner, & M. J. Furlong (Eds.), *Handbook of positive psychology in schools* (pp. 131–145). New York: Routledge.

Singleton, G. E., & Linton, C. (2006). *Courageous conversations about race: A field guide for achieving equity in schools.* Thousand Oaks, CA: Corwin Press.

Snell, M. (Interviewer). (1999, September 1). Innovator: Judy Kranzler. *Blueprint Magazine.* Accessed at www.dlc.org/ndol_ci.cfm?kaid=110&subid=181&contentid=1234 on August 24, 2010.

Snoeyink, R. (2009). *Using video self-analysis to improve withitness of student teachers.* Paper presented at International Society for Computing in Education National Educational Computing Conference (NECC) 2009 Annual Conference, Washington, DC. Accessed at www.iste.org/Content/NavigationMenu/Research/NECC_Research_Paper_Archives/NECC2009/Snoeyink_NECC09.pdf on August 24, 2010.

Sousa, D. (1998). *Learning manual for how the brain learns.* Thousand Oaks, CA: Corwin Press.

Stafford, T. (2009, January 19). *Learning should be fun.* Accessed at http://schoolofeverything.com/blog/learning-should-be-fun on January 25, 2010.

Sternberg, R., & Williams, W. M. (1998). *Teaching for creativity: Two dozen tips.* Accessed at www.cdl.org/resource-library/articles/teaching_creativity.php on November 23, 2009.

Strong, R., Silver, H., Perini, M., & Tuculescu, G. (2003). Boredom and its opposite. *Educational Leadership, 61*(1), 24–29.

Tatum, B. D. (2007). *Can we talk about race? And other conversations in an era of school resegregation.* Boston: Beacon Press.

Teachnology. (2009). *The effects of poverty on teaching and learning.* Bloomingburg, NY: Author. Accessed at www.teach-nology.com/tutorials/teaching/poverty/ on January 13, 2010.

Tomlinson, C. A. (2004). *How to differentiate instruction in mixed-ability classrooms.* Alexandria, VA: Association for Supervision and Curriculum Development.

Toppo, G. (2003, July 2). The face of the American teacher: White and female while her students are ethnically diverse. *USA TODAY*. Accessed at www.teachforamerica.org/assets/documents/070203_USAToday _FaceOfAmericanTeacher.pdf on December 17, 2009.

Trei, L. (February 7, 2007). New study yields instructive results on how mindset affects learning. *Stanford Report*. Accessed at http://newsservice.stanford .edu/news/2007/february7/dweck-020707.html on October 15, 2009.

Trudeau, M. (2007, February 15). Students' view of intelligence can help grades. On *Morning Edition*. Washington, DC: National Public Radio. Accessed at www .npr.org/templates/story/story.php?storyId=7406521 on October 5, 2009.

Tulsa Initiative Blog. (2009, February 25). *I like school better with grandmas and grandpas—Liam*. Accessed at http://tulsainitiative.wordpress .com/2009/02/25/i-like-school-better-with-grandmas-and-grandpas-liam/ on January 11, 2010.

Turner, J. H., & Stets, J. E. (2005). *The sociology of emotions*. Cambridge, UK: Cambridge University Press.

U.S. Department of Education. (2009, November). *Race to the top program executive summary*. Washington, DC: Author.

U.S. Department of Education, Office of Planning, Evaluation, and Policy Development, Policy and Program Studies Service. (2009). *Evaluation of evidence-based practices in online learning: A meta-analysis and review of online learning studies*. Washington, DC: Author.

Vakos, P. (2010). Why the blank stare? Strategies for visual learners. Accessed at www.phschool.com/eteach/social_studies/2003_05/essay.html on August 12, 2010.

Walsh, B. (2005). *Unleashing your brilliance*. Victoria, Canada: Walsh Seminars Ltd. Accessed at www.walshseminars.com/UYBeBOOK.pdf on August 24, 2010.

Weinstein, M. (1996). *Managing to have fun: How fun at work can motivate your employees, inspire your coworkers, boost your bottom line*. New York: Fireside Press.

Wilen, W. W. (1992). *Questions, questioning techniques and effective teaching* (3rd ed.). Washington, DC: NEA Professional Library, National Education Association.

Wilson, S. (2004). Creative projects stimulate classroom learning. *Science Scope*, *28*(2), 41–43.

Wolfe, P. (2001). *Brain matters: Translating research into classroom practice.* Alexandria, VA: Association for Supervision and Curriculum Development.

Wood, W. (2009). *Neuro Newes, 14, 15, 16, 17, 18.* Columbia, MO.

Wubbels, T., & Brekelmans, M. (2005). Two decades of research on teacher-student relationships in class. *International Journal of Educational Research, 43*(1–2), 6–24.

Yatvin, J. (2000). Minority view. In National Reading Panel, *Teaching children to read: An evidence-based assessment of the scientific research literature on reading and its implications for reading instruction: Reports of the subgroups.* Rockville, MD: National Institute of Child Health and Human Development. Accessed at www.nichd.nih.gov/publications/nrp/report.cfm on January 12, 2010.

Yatvin, J. (2007). 2007 NCTE presidential address: Where ignorant armies clash by night. *Council Chronicle, 17*(4), 25–31.

Yazzie-Mintz, E. (2007). *Voices of students on engagement: A report on the 2006 high school survey of student engagement.* Bloomington, IN: Center for Evaluation and Education Policy. Accessed at www.eric .ed.gov/ERICWebPortal/custom/portlets/recordDetails/detailmini.jsp?_nfpb =true&_&ERICExtSearch_SearchValue_0=ED495758&ERICExtSearch_ SearchType_0=no&accno=ED495758 on October 20, 2009.

Yazzie-Mintz, E. (2009, December 6). *Engaging all students for greater learning and achievement.* Presentation given at NSDC's 41st Annual Conference, St. Louis, Missouri.

Yerkes, L. (2007). *Fun works: Creating places where people love to work.* San Francisco: Berrett-Koehler Publishers, Inc.

Yusuf, H. (2008, September 18). Video games start to shape classroom curriculum. *Christian Science Monitor.* Accessed at www.csmonitor.com/Innovation /Tech-Culture/2008/0918/video-games-start-to-shape-classroom-curricu- lum on December 1, 2009.

Zemelman, S., Daniels, H., & Hyde, A. (2005). *Best practice: Today's standards for teaching and learning in America's schools* (3rd ed.). Portsmouth, NH: Heinemann.

Zernitsky, L. (2004). SIS Image #7136700056. *Educational Leadership, 62*(2), 80.

INDEX

Motivating Students Who Don't Care: Successful Techniques for Educators
Allen N. Mendler
Proven strategies and five effective processes empower you to reawaken motivation in students who aren't prepared, don't care, and won't work.
BKF360

Motivating Students: 25 Strategies to Light the Fire of Engagement
Carolyn Chapman and Nicole Vagle
Learn why students disengage and how to motivate them to achieve success with a five-step framework. Research-based strategies and fun activities, along with tips and troubleshooting strategies, show how to instill a lasting love of learning in students of any age.
BKF371

Creating a Digital-Rich Classroom: Teaching & Learning in a Web 2.0 World
Meg Ormiston
Design and deliver standards-based lessons in which technology plays an integral role. This book provides a research base and practical strategies for using Web 2.0 tools to create engaging lessons that transform and enrich content.
BKF385

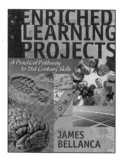

Enriched Learning Projects: A Practical Pathway to 21st Century Skills
James Bellanca
Foreword by Bob Pearlman
Translate standards-based content into enriched learning projects that build 21st century skills. This book also highlights e-tools that enhance learning projects and offers research-based instructional strategies.
BKF296

Solution Tree | Press a division of
Solution Tree
Visit solution-tree.com or call 800.733.6786 to order.